LEADING
LITTLE
ONES
TO
GOD

Leading Little Ones to God

Marian M. Schoolland

ILLUSTRATIONS BY PAUL STOUB

A CHILD'S BOOK OF BIBLE TEACHINGS

WM. B. EERDMANS PUBLISHING COMPANY, Grand Rapids, Michigan

Text © 1962, 1981 Wm. B. Eerdmans Publishing Company
Artwork © 1981 Paul Stoub

Published 1962 by Wm. B Eerdmans Publishing Company
2140 Oak Industrial Dr. NE, Grand Rapids, Michigan 49505
Revised edition 1981
Paperback edition 1995

Manufactured at Worzalla in USA in June 2012, twentieth edition

12 13 14 15 16 17 18   27 26 25 24 23 22 21 20

Library of Congress catalog card number 62-11250

ISBN-13: 978-0-8028-5120-8

The publisher gratefully acknowledges permission to reprint stanzas of the following hymn texts:

"A Prayer" ("Be Thou My Vision"), from *The Poem Book of the Gael,* selected and edited by Eleanor Hull; used by permission of the Editor's Literary Estate and Chatto & Windus Ltd.

"Jesus Lead the Way," from *The Hymnal 1940* © The Church Pension Fund.

"Come Jesus, Holy Child, to Me," from *Children's Hymnal*, Concordia Publishing House.

"In Adam We Have All Been One," from *Joyful Sounds* © 1977 by Concordia Publishing House.

"Because of Thy Great Bounty" ("Because I Have Been Given Much"), from *Poems of Inspiration and Courage* by Grace Noll Crowell © 1930, 1934 by Harper and Row Publishers, Inc., renewed © 1958 by Grace Noll Crowell; used by permission of the publishers.

"Wake Us, O Lord, to Human Need," © Phyllis Kersten.

"O Dearest Lord, Thy Sacred Head," by Father Andrew; from *Mirfield Mission Hymn Book*, A. R. Mowbray and Co. Ltd.

"Dear Lord, Here in Thy House of Prayer," © The National Society.

"Far Above in Highest Heaven" and "Seek Ye First the Kingdom," from *Congregational Praise* © The United Reformed Church.

"O God, Thou Faithful God," from *Geer's Hymnal for Colleges and Schools* © Yale University Press.

Suffer the little children to come unto me,
and forbid them not:
for of such is the kingdom of God.
MARK 10:14

These words, which I command thee this day, shall be in thine heart:
and thou shalt teach them diligently unto thy children,
and shalt talk of them when thou sittest in thine house,
and when thou walkest by the way,
and when thou liest down,
and when thou risest up.
DEUTERONOMY 6:6, 7

Acknowledgments

I wish to express my appreciation for the help I received in the construction of this book. Marian Ippel kindly tried out the first lesson in her family circle, and encouraged me to continue with the work. Charlotte Otten read the entire manuscript and made valuable comments. And my very special thanks goes to my brother, the Reverend C. M. Schoolland, who offered detailed suggestions based on his years of experience with children. I am also grateful to the publishers, who kindly permitted me to combine my ideas for a devotional book with their plan of producing a doctrinal book. Above all, we cannot be thankful enough to our God, who so revealed Himself that even a small child can grasp something of His majesty, holiness, and love.

— *M.M.S.*

A Word to Parents

This book is intended to be a guide to parents who desire to teach their little ones about God. Parents are the child's best teachers, and perhaps there is nothing more important in his or her spiritual development than quiet talks with Mother or Father about the great God who made us and loves us.

Little children enjoy being read to. This can be done almost any time of the day, although it is best to reserve it for a regularly recurring quiet period, such as after the last mealtime of the day, during family devotions, or at bedtime. Material such as this requires thinking on their part; therefore it should be read slowly so that the children's minds can take it in. Spacings and italics have been used to help make the reading most meaningful.

There are questions included to suggest subjects for conversation. They will help the parents to understand the child's thinking and the child to apply the teachings of the Bible to his or her own small affairs.

A small child cannot be expected to memorize all the Bible verses, but repetition of the given verses, along with discussion and explanation, makes for a groundwork of familiarity. And the older children will enjoy committing at least parts of the verses to memory.

The suggested Bible passages are perhaps better omitted when the children are very young. Older children will enjoy having the lesson confirmed by words from the Bible itself.

Since singing is a stimulus and inspiration to Christian living, as well as an expression of faith and joy, we hope that parents and children will sing the suggested songs together. Singing is a lovely way of praising God and of strengthening our faith and trust. Often a little talk about the meaning of the hymn will help. If a hymn tune is not familiar, the words can be read and used for discussion.*

Prayer is a precious means of sealing to the child's heart the seed that has just been sown. The prayers suggested at the end of the lesson may be used as given, or may serve merely as a guide in applying the subject matter of the lesson.

This book is sent forth with the prayer that it may be a blessing in every home where it is used to the honor of God, and that little ones, such as Jesus took into His arms, may learn to know and love Him.

—MARIAN M. SCHOOLLAND

*The hymn tunes have been cross-referenced to three popular and readily available children's hymnals:
CH—*The Children's Hymnbook* (Grand Rapids: National Union of Christian Schools and Eerdmans, 1962)
HY—*Hymns for Youth* (Grand Rapids: National Union of Christian Schools and Eerdmans, 1966)
JS—*Joyful Sounds* (St. Louis: Concordia Publishing House, 1977)
The tune names have been provided so that readers can locate the tunes in other hymnbooks that may be in their homes.

CONTENTS

PART ONE

●

Looking
For
God

Our Hearts Ask for God

This is a book about *God*. It is also about people, and about everything we see all around us. But it is about *God* most of all.

It is about God most of all because everybody should know God. God is very important. He made us. We belong to Him. The whole world belongs to Him, and the sun and the moon, and all the millions of stars that twinkle far, far above us. All this belongs to Him. Don't you think we ought to know Him?

Deep down in every heart there is a little voice that tells us that there is a God and that we ought to know Him. Some people do not listen to that little voice; they do not want to know God. Some people listen, but make their own gods. People have made gods of wood and stone. Some have prayed to the sun and the stars, as if they were gods. But such gods cannot hear us, or see us, or help us in any way at all. We want to know the *true* God, who *sees* us and *hears* us and can *help* us when we need Him.

Did you ever see a baby reach up its arms to its mother? The baby needs its mother and wants its mother. Mother takes care of her baby. A good mother takes care of all her children. We are God's children because He made us: we belong to Him. And we *need* Him to take care of us. This book was written to help little children find God, and know Him, and love Him. As we read this book we will talk about God:

how great He is;
how wonderful and good He is;
how much He loves us;
how He takes care of us;
what He wants us to do;
and much more.

To *know God* is really the most important thing in all the world! It will make us really happy. When we know Him, we will love Him, we will trust Him, and we will obey Him.

SOMETHING TO TALK ABOUT:
What does the little voice deep down in our hearts tell us?
What are some of the wonderful things God made?
Why do we need God?

MEMORY VERSE
Long ago God said:
Seek ye the Lord while He may be found.
ISAIAH 55:6

3

That is what we want to do as we read this book.

SUGGESTED READING:
Psalm 105:1–4

HYMN
Here is a song to sing about God:

> Who made ocean, earth, and sky?
>   God, our loving Father.
> Who made sun and moon on high?
>   God, our loving Father.
> Who made all the birds that fly?
>   God, our loving Father.
>
> Who made lakes and rivers blue?

God, our loving Father.
Who made snow and rain and dew?
  God, our loving Father.
He made little children too,
  God, our loving Father.

FINNISH MELODY
(CH 11)

PRAYER
(Shall we ask God to help us learn about Him through reading this book?)

God in heaven, we are glad that we may pray to Thee. We ask Thee to bless us as we read this book together. We want to learn more and more about Thee, so that we will love Thee very much. *Amen.*

We Cannot
See God

Would you like to see God? Yes. But we *cannot* see God. *Nobody* has ever seen God.

Why can we not see God?

We cannot see God because He is *spirit*. We cannot *see* a spirit.

What *is* a spirit?

Well, when God made you, He gave you a body and a *spirit*, or soul. Your spirit lives inside your body. Your spirit is the real *you*. It is your *spirit*, inside your body, that listens while we read; it is your spirit that thinks and loves: it is your spirit that is happy and makes you smile;

it is your spirit that is sad sometimes and makes the tears come.

Nobody can *see* your spirit. But you can feel it living there, inside of you.

Now God is *all* spirit. He does not have a body. That is why we cannot see Him. But He sees and hears and loves; He sees and hears *much more* than we can see or hear, even though *we* cannot see Him.

There is a reason, too, why we *must* not see God. God is all glorious. That means that He is very holy and shiny bright.

4

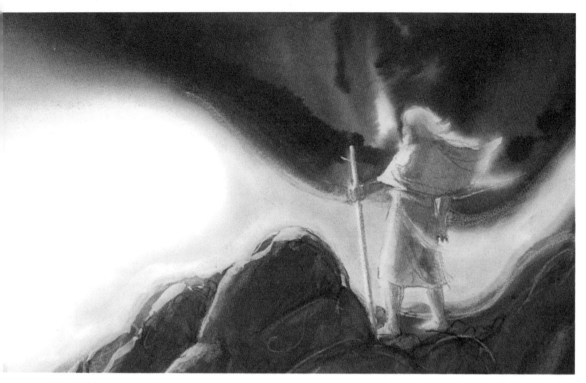

The Bible tells us about a man named Moses. Moses was a good friend of God. God often talked to Moses. But Moses *never saw* God.

One day Moses said to God, "Please, show me Your glory."

God said to Moses, "No man can see Me and live. But I will hide you in the rocks, and then I will pass by you."

Moses went up on a mountain alone. God hid him between the rocks, and God passed by him. God let Moses see just a *little bit* of His glory. Even a man like Moses could not stand to see more than that of God's glory.

When Moses came down from the mountain, his face was bright as sunshine. Just seeing a *little* of God's glory had made his face shine so bright that the people were afraid of him.

The glory of God is so bright that nobody could *bear* to see Him. We cannot bear to look at the sun when it shines bright. It hurts our eyes to look at the sun. God's glory is much greater than the glory of the sun.

It is *good* that we cannot see God.

The sunshine and the stars tell us about His glory. But if we *saw* Him, or even *part* of His glory, we would be very afraid. We could not even live!

SOMETHING TO TALK ABOUT:
Has anybody ever seen God?
Why is it that we cannot see God?
Why would it not be good for us to see God?

GOD SAID TO MOSES:
There shall no man see me, and live.

EXODUS 33:20

SUGGESTED READING:
Psalm 104:1–13

THIS IS A BEAUTIFUL HYMN ABOUT GOD:
My God, how wonderful Thou art,
Thy majesty how bright!
How beautiful Thy mercy-seat
In depths of burning light!

ST. ETHELDREDA
(HY 12)

(Even though God is so glorious, we may pray to Him. Shall we close our eyes and bow our heads, so that we will think only about Him while we pray?)

God of glory, brighter than the sun, help us to praise Thee. Make us pure and sinless, through Jesus our Saviour, so that we need not be afraid of Thee. *Amen.*

We See God's Works

There is so much to see all around us! There is so much to learn!

Do you know *how* we learn?

We learn by seeing and by hearing.

Can we learn about *God* that way? We cannot *see* Him. We do not hear Him talk to us. Then how can we *learn* about Him? How can we *know* Him?

We can know Him through the things He made.

Did you ever look at the stars, shining bright in the sky?

Do you often look around at the earth, so big and wide? There are so many wonderful things on the earth—furry animals, birds, flowers, and little bugs. There are big wide oceans of water, with thousands of big fish and little fish.

Who made all this?

Who takes care of all this?

Somebody must have made it all. That Somebody is *God*.

Sometimes we hear the thunder roar, and we see the lightning flash. You and I cannot make thunder and lightning. We cannot make clouds and rain. We cannot make the wind blow, and we cannot *stop* the wind when it blows. All these things that we cannot do tell us that there is a great God. He makes the thunder and lightning. He makes the wind, and the rain, and the pretty snowflakes.

Sometimes we hear a little bird sing. We cannot give a little bird a sweet song to sing. We cannot teach him how to make his little nest. When we see a little bird fly and hear him sing, we know there is a great *God* who made birds.

Flowers are very pretty. They have pretty petals. There are all kinds of flowers—blue ones and yellow ones and red ones. Some have a drop of honey-water deep down in their throats. Some have sweet perfume in their petals. Look at a flower very carefully and see how beautiful it is. And think of the living seeds that flowers make. *We* cannot make even *one* real flower, with a drop of honey-water in its throat and sweet perfume in its petals. Only *God* can. So the flowers tell us there is a God.

We *know* there is a God because we can see what He has done. We see the things *He* has made.

SOMETHING TO TALK ABOUT:

How do the sun and moon and stars tell you there is a God?

Can you name some other things that tell us there is a God?

THE BIBLE SAYS:

The heavens declare the glory of God.

PSALM 19:1

SUGGESTED READING:

Psalm 19:1–7

WE CAN SING PSALM 19:

The spacious heavens declare
The glory of our God,
The firmament displays
His handiwork abroad;
Day unto day proclaims His might,
And night His wisdom tells to night.

ARTHUR'S SEAT

NOW SHALL WE PRAY TO GOD?

O God, when we look all around us, we see that Thou art a very great God. When we look up at the sky, the heavens tell us that Thou art great. When we look around us, the birds and flowers tell us how wonderful Thou art. We are so small! But we belong to Thee. And we know Thou wilt take care of us for Jesus' sake. *Amen.*

God Talked to People Long Ago

Adam and Eve were the very first people God made—a man and a woman, just those two. After God made Adam and Eve, He used to talk to them. In the evening, when the sun was going down, He came to the garden to talk to them.

Many years later, God talked to a man named Abraham. Abraham was God's *friend*.

God talked to Moses, too. God talked to Moses

7

many times. Once Moses was up on Mount Sinai with God for forty days. Moses did not even have to eat, because God took care of Him while He talked to him.

The Bible also tells us how God talked to a *little boy* one night. This little boy lived in God's tabernacle. His name was Samuel.

Samuel helped Eli, the old priest, take care of God's tabernacle. One night God talked to Samuel.

Samuel was in bed. God called, "Samuel! Samuel!"

Samuel thought that Eli was calling him. He jumped out of bed and ran to Eli. But Eli said, "No, I did not call you." Samuel went back to bed.

God called Samuel again—"Samuel! Samuel!" Samuel thought, "It *must* be Eli calling me." But when he ran to Eli, Eli said, "No, my son, I did not call you." And Samuel went back to bed again.

But then he heard the Voice *again*—"Samuel! Samuel!"

Samuel ran to Eli once more. This time Eli said, "Now I know who is calling you. It is the *Lord!* Go back to bed. And if you hear His voice

again, you must say, 'Speak, Lord, and I will listen.' "

Samuel lay down once again. He could hardly believe that God would *really* talk to him. He was only a little boy. He lay very still. He listened. And then—then he heard the Voice *again*—"Samuel! Samuel!"

And he said, "Speak, Lord. I will listen!"

God talked to Samuel that night. He told him things that were going to happen.

After that, God talked to Samuel many times. Samuel became one of the great *prophets*. He told people what God wanted them to do.

God has talked to many others. They were His prophets too. God sent them to tell His word to His people.

SOMETHING TO TALK ABOUT:
Can you name two men that God talked to?
At what time of day did God call Samuel?
Did Samuel *see* God?
What did Samuel say to God?

MEMORY VERSE
If we should ever hear the voice of God, we should say what Samuel said:

Speak, Lord; for thy servant heareth.

I SAMUEL 3:9

SUGGESTED READING:
I Samuel 3:1–10

HYMN
This hymn is a prayer that says we should always be ready to speak to God:

Be Thou my vision, O Lord of my heart;
Nought be all else to me save that Thou
    art.
Thou my best thought, by day or by night,
Waking or sleeping, Thy presence my light.

Be Thou my wisdom, and Thou my true
    word;
I ever with Thee and Thou with me, Lord,

Thou my great Father, I Thy true son;
Thou in me dwelling, and I with Thee one.

SLANE
(HY 103; JS 78)

A PRAYER:

Help us, dear Father, to be like little Samuel, to listen when we hear Your voice. *Amen.*

5

God Talks to Us

We talk to God when we *pray* to Him. We close our eyes. We think about God. And then we *talk* to Him. And we *know* that He hears us, because He is all around us.

But does God talk to *us?* Can *we* hear Him?

Long ago He talked to little Samuel. He talked to many others. But does He talk to you and to me?

Yes, He does talk to us. He talks to us in several ways. He talks to us through His book most of all.

When God talked to men long ago, He told them to *write down* His words. He told them to write His words in a book. They made a big book. We call this book the *Bible.* The Bible is God's Word.

God took care of the Bible. Though it was written many, many years ago, we can read it *today.* He took care of it because *He wanted to talk to you and me through the Bible.*

When we *read* the Bible, God is talking to us.

When the minister reads the Bible to us, God is talking to us.

When Father and Mother read the Bible to us, God is talking to us.

When our teachers read the Bible to us, and tell us the Bible stories, God is talking to us.

There are many, many books in the world. The *Bible* is the most wonderful of them all. The Bible, the *whole* Bible, is God talking to us.

We love the Bible because it is God's Word.

We take care of our Bibles.

We read our Bibles often, because we want to know what God says to us.

God talked to us in a very *special* way when He sent *Jesus,* His Son, to live on earth. Many of the things that Jesus said are also in the Bible.

And God talks to us when *His Spirit* whispers in our hearts. Sometimes the Spirit whispers to tell us not to be naughty. Sometimes the Spirit whispers when we are praying, to tell us that God hears us.

Even though we do not hear the voice of God

9

with our *ears,* as Samuel did, God *does* talk to us. He talks to us in many ways.

SOMETHING TO TALK ABOUT:
In what book does God talk to us?
Who wrote this book?
Why is the Bible the most wonderful of all books?

MEMORY VERSE
When we memorize parts of the Bible, we hide God's words in our hearts. Long ago a man of God said:

Thy word have I hid in mine heart, that I might not sin against thee.

PSALM 119:11

SUGGESTED READING:
I Peter 1:24, 25

AND HERE IS A HYMN ABOUT GOD'S WORD:
Almighty God, Your Word is cast
Like seed into the ground;
Now let the dew of heav'n descend
And righteous fruits abound.

DUNDEE
(JS 71)

PRAYER
(The song we just sang is a prayer. Shall we close our eyes and say the words softly, to God?)

Amen.

God Sent His Son

In our last lesson we learned how God told men to write a book, the Bible. God gave us the Bible so that we can *learn* about Him and *know* Him. God *talks* to us through the Bible. It is a wonderful book!

But God wanted us to know Him even better. He wanted us to know Him not only as the God who *made* us, but as the heavenly Father who *loves* us. He sent Jesus, His Son, down to earth.

When Jesus came to earth the angels in heaven sang for joy. One of them came down to earth to tell some shepherds that they could find Jesus, God's Son, in a stable! He was a baby then. Do you know what day that was?

Jesus came to God's special people, the Israelites. They are often called Jews. When Jesus was grown up, He walked all through their country. He told the people about God and God's great Kingdom. He told them that God loves us. Wherever Jesus went He did good. He healed the sick. He made the blind see. He gave food to the hungry. He was a friend to those who were sorry for their sin.

10

One day, when Jesus was talking to His disciples about His Father in heaven, Philip said to Him, "Lord, *show* us the Father."

Jesus said, "I have been with you a long time, Philip; you know *Me*, don't you? Well, if you have seen *Me*, you have seen the *Father!*"

What did Jesus mean?

Why, He meant to tell Philip, and to tell you and me, that God, our Father in heaven, is *just like Jesus*, His Son!

Now, we know that Jesus was very good and kind. He did great and wonderful things, too—healing the sick, making the blind see, and sometimes even raising up the dead to live again! When Jesus did such things, He showed us how good and kind, and how great and wonderful God the *Father* is.

These stories about Jesus are written in the Bible—in the New Testament part of the Bible. So reading the *Bible* is still the best way of learning to know about God. We learn about Him by *seeing* what He *made*—the earth and the heavens and everything that is on earth or up in the sky. But we learn to know God *best* of all by reading His *book*, the Bible. That tells us what He said to men of long ago. And it tells us about all the wonderful things Jesus did. He even died for us!

When we think how much Jesus loved us, we must remember that God the Father, up in heaven, loves us *just* as much. We can be *sure* about that, because Jesus said:

I and my Father are one (John 10:30).

SOMETHING TO TALK ABOUT:

How did Jesus show us that God is good and kind?

How did He show us that God feels sorry for the sick?

How did He show us that God loves sinners?

What is most wonderful about Christmas?

SUGGESTED READING:

John 14:8–10

HYMN

We are glad that Jesus showed us how good and kind God the Father is. We can sing about His loving care:

How strong and sweet my Father's care
That round about me, like the air,
Is with me always, everywhere!
He cares for me.

O keep me ever in Thy love,
Dear Father, watching from above,
And as through life my steps shall move,
O care for me.

ES IST KEIN TAG
(HY 35)

PRAYER

(Shall we thank God for showing us His love in Jesus?)

Dear Father in heaven, we thank Thee for sending Jesus. He was good and kind. He showed us how good Thou art. Help us to know Thee better, through Jesus Christ, Thy Son. *Amen.*

MEMORY VERSES OF PART ONE

Seek ye the Lord while He may be found.
ISAIAH 55:6

There shall no man see me, and live.
EXODUS 33:20

The heavens declare the glory of God.
PSALM 19:1

Speak Lord; for thy servant heareth.
I SAMUEL 3:9

Thy word have I hid in mine heart, that I might not sin against thee.
PSALM 119:11

I and my Father are one.
JOHN 10:30

PART TWO

·

God
Is
Very Great

God Is One God

Did you ever wish you had wings like a bird, so that you could fly? If you had wings, would you like to fly up and up and up, high into the sky, to see all the *stars?*

If you went on and on and on, for days and days, you *still* would not see *all* the stars. There are so *many!* Millions and millions of them!

God made all those stars. He made every one of them. And He made everything else that you see.

Many years ago the Israelites were God's people. There were many people on earth, but God chose the Israelites to be His very special people. He talked to them through Moses. He gave them a beautiful country to live in. He told them that God is God *alone.* There are no other gods, and so they must worship only Him.

People who lived around the land of Israel thought there were many gods—one who made the stars, one who made the moon, one who lived in the ocean. They also made idol gods of wood and stone.

Sometimes even God's own people, who knew how wonderful and good God is, forgot about Him; *they* made idols and prayed to them.

One day God sent them a prophet named Isaiah, to tell them how foolish they were. Isaiah said, "Listen. I will tell you how foolish you are.

A man goes to the woods with his ax. He finds a good tree and cuts it down. He chops it to pieces. He uses some of the wood to make a fire.

"When he has a fire burning, he says, 'Ah, this is a nice warm fire.'

"Then he takes a piece of the same tree home. He cuts and carves it and makes it look like a man, with ears and eyes and nose and a mouth. He puts shining gold over it. And he says, 'There! I have made me a god!' He kneels down to that piece of wood, to that piece of a tree!

"What a foolish man he is! That piece of wood cannot *hear.* It cannot *see.* It cannot even *move.* It is an idol. It did not make the earth and the sky. It did not make the stars. It cannot send rain."

Isaiah told the people that there is only *one* true God. He made *all* things. He alone is *Lord* over all things. Everything *belongs* to Him. *He* takes care of everything.

We cannot see Him, because He is *spirit.* But He is the God who hears us when we pray. He is *very great.*

SOMETHING TO TALK ABOUT:

Why is it foolish to make idol gods?
To whom do earth and sky belong?

14

Why do all things belong to Him?
Why do we belong to Him?

MOSES TOLD GOD'S PEOPLE OF LONG AGO:
The Lord he is God in heaven above, and upon the earth beneath.

DEUTERONOMY 4:39

SUGGESTED READING:
Deuteronomy 6:4–7

A HYMN TO SING:
We all believe in one true God,
Father, Son, and Holy Ghost,

Everpresent Help in need,
Praised by all the heav'nly host,
By whose mighty pow'r alone
All is made and wrought and done.

WIR GLAUBEN ALL' AN EINEN GOTT
(HY 120; JS 119)

A PRAYER:
Father in heaven, we will pray only to You, because You are the one true God. We know You hear us when we pray. We know You have all things in Your hand—the little birds, and the big shining sun, and us too. *Amen.*

God Is Everywhere

God is *everywhere!*

When we look around, we cannot see God. But He is *here.* And He is over *there.* He is close beside us, and He is high above us too, in heaven. And He is far away on the other side of the earth!

Because God is *God,* and because He is a *Spirit,* He can be *everywhere* at the *same time.* God is very, very great!

The Bible tells us about a young woman named Hagar. She was a slave. Sarah, the wife of Abraham, was her mistress. One day Hagar ran away from her mistress, because her mistress was not kind to her. Hagar went far away,

to a strange place. She thought nobody loved her. She was very unhappy. She sat down by a well of water. And she thought she was all alone.

But she was *not* alone. *God* was there. He saw her. He knew her trouble. He knew her heart was very sad. And He loved her.

Suddenly Hagar heard God talk to her! God said, "Hagar, go back to your mistress. Do what she tells you to do. I will take care of you."

Hagar was *so* surprised! She said, "I did not think that God would see me *here!* But He did see me!"

Hagar was glad. She obeyed God. She went back to her mistress, and God took care of her.

15

It made Hagar *happy* to know that God saw her. She had been so sad, and she had thought she was all alone. But God saw her *all the time.*

It should make *us* happy to think that God is everywhere, that He sees us, and that we are never alone.

When you go to bed at night, God is there. The room may be dark, but you do not have to be afraid. When you walk to school alone, you are not *really* alone. God is there. He is with you. Doesn't it make you *happy* to know He is everywhere?

It should make us *careful,* too, to think that God is always everywhere.

When you are playing, God is there. He sees what you do. He hears what you say. If we *remember* that, we will be very careful to say and do only what pleases Him.

It should make us *wonder* to think that God is everywhere.

You can be in only one place at a time. If you are at home, you are not in school. If you are here, in this room, you are not outdoors. But *God* is everywhere. Look up at the big wide sky. Look up at the stars. Look all around you. Think, "God is *everywhere! Everywhere!*" How wonderful God is!

SOMETHING TO TALK ABOUT:
How can God be everywhere?
Why should it make us happy to know He is
    always everywhere?

GOD TELLS US THAT HE IS EVERYWHERE:
Do not I fill heaven and earth? saith the Lord.
JEREMIAH 23:24

SUGGESTED READING:
Psalm 95:1–6

THIS IS A HAPPY HYMN:
    None is like God, who reigns above,
    So great, so pure, so high;
    None is like God, whose name is love,
    And who is always nigh.

In all the earth there is no spot
Excluded from His care;
We cannot go where God is not,
For He is everywhere.
OLD GOTHLAND MELODY
(CH 14)

PRAYER
(Let us fold our hands and talk to God):

O God, it makes us happy to think that You are always with us; that You always see us. Help us to remember that You are very near. *Amen.*

God Knows All Things

Boys and girls go to school as soon as they are old enough. They go to school to *learn*. There is so *much* to learn.

But God never goes to school. God does not have to learn. God *knows* all things.

God knows things that we cannot know. He knows how many stars there are up in the sky. He calls the stars by their names.

God knows things we cannot *see*. He knows how the big trees push their roots into the ground, and how they send water up through the stems to each little leaf.

God knows all that happens *in the dark*. Nobody can hide from Him, not even in the darkest night.

God knows all that is in our *hearts,* too. He knows what we *think*. He knows *every* secret. God knows *all things*.

The Bible tells us about a great king, Nebuchadnezzar. Nebuchadnezzar had a strange dream one night. When he awoke, he could not remember his dream. That made him unhappy.

The king sent for his wise men. He said to them, "Tell me my dream!" But they could not tell the king his dream. How could *they* know the king's dream? Then the king was angry.

Daniel was one of the king's wise men. Daniel said, "I will ask *God* to tell me the king's dream."

Daniel said, "God knows all secret things. *He* knows even what is in the darkness. He knows even our dreams." Daniel prayed to God and God told Daniel the king's dream. God knew it all the time. And then Daniel told it to the king.

God even knows everything that is *going to happen*. We make plans. We say, "Tomorrow I will go out and play," or, "Tomorrow I will go to school." But we are not *sure* of what we shall do tomorrow. *Only* God knows for sure what will happen tomorrow, and the next day, and next year. . . .

God is *very great*. He knows *all things*.

SOMETHING TO TALK ABOUT:
Why do boys and girls go to school?
Does God have to learn things?
How much does God know about you and me?

MEMORY VERSE
A part of the Bible is called the book of Psalms. The Psalms were written long ago. Psalm 139 tells us that God knows *every little thing* about you and me. The man who wrote Psalm 139 said to God:

Thou knowest my downsitting and mine uprising.

PSALM 139:2

Do you know what that means?

SUGGESTED READING:
Psalm 139:1–10

WE CAN SING THAT PSALM:
O Lord, my inmost heart and thought
Thy searching eye doth see;
Where'er I rest, where'er I go,
My ways are known to Thee.

BINGHAM

SHALL WE PRAY TO GOD?
O Lord, it is wonderful to think that You know all things! You see my heart when I am naughty. You see me when I try to be good. Help me, dear Father, to be good for Jesus' sake, because He loves me so! *Amen.*

God Is
Three Persons

God is so *very* great that we shall *never* know all about Him. We cannot understand God.

The Bible tells us that God is *One*. We have learned that there is *only one* God. But the Bible also tells us that God is *three*. God is three Per-sons, yet He is one *God*. That is something we cannot understand.

The Bible tells us about God the Father, and about God the Son, and about God the Holy Spirit. *They* are the three Persons.

18

God the Father is in heaven.

Jesus is *God the Son.* Jesus came to this earth as a baby. We remember His birthday on Christmas.

God the Holy Spirit came down to be with Jesus. He came when Jesus was baptized. And afterwards He came again, to live in the hearts of those who believe in Jesus.

There was a man named John, who baptized people in the river. People called him John the Baptist. One day Jesus went to John the Baptist. Jesus wanted to be baptized.

John and Jesus went down into the water together. John baptized Jesus. When they came out of the water, John saw something wonderful. Something that looked like a *dove* came down from heaven. It came and rested right on Jesus' head.

It was not *really* a dove. It was God the Holy Spirit in the *form* of a dove.

At the same time John heard a voice. The voice said, "This is my beloved Son!" That was the voice of God the *Father. He* spoke from heaven.

In this way God showed himself in the *three Persons.* Jesus, God the Son, was baptized. God the Holy Spirit came down like a dove. And God the Father spoke from heaven. So all three Persons were there: the Father, the Son, and the Holy Spirit. How wonderful and great God is!

Sometimes the Holy Spirit is called the Holy Ghost. When somebody is baptized today, he is baptized in the name of the Father, and of the Son, and of the Holy Ghost, because God is three Persons.

SOMETHING TO TALK ABOUT:
Is there more than one God?

Who is God the Son?

What did God the Father do when Jesus was baptized?

What did God the Holy Spirit do when Jesus was baptized?

LONG AGO A PSALM WRITER WROTE:
Great is the Lord, and greatly to be praised.

PSALM 145:3

SUGGESTED READING:
Matthew 28:16–20

HYMN

We sometimes sing this hymn in church. When we sing it we praise the Father, the Son, and the Holy Spirit:

Praise God, from whom all blessings flow:
Praise Him, all creatures here below;
Praise Him above, ye heav'nly host;
Praise Father, Son, and Holy Ghost.

OLD HUNDREDTH
(CH 25; JS 102)

PRAYER
(Shall we praise all three Persons now, as we pray to God?)

Father, we praise Thee, for Thou art very great. Jesus, we thank Thee for coming to earth to be our Saviour. Holy Spirit, come and live with us, and make us children of God. *Amen.*

19

God
Is Holy

Isaiah was one of God's great prophets. God often spoke to Isaiah. He told Isaiah to tell God's people that someday a wonderful Saviour would come.

One day God spoke to Isaiah in a vision. A vision is something like a dream. In that vision Isaiah saw the Lord sitting upon a throne, high up. His robe filled the Temple. And above Him there were *seraphim*. Seraphim are shining heavenly creatures.

Isaiah saw that each of the seraphim had six wings. With two wings he covered his face, with two he covered his feet, and he used two to fly.

These wonderful seraphim called to each other. One said, *"Holy, holy, holy, is the Lord of hosts: the whole earth is full of his glory."* Then another answered, *"Holy, holy, holy!"*

When Isaiah saw the vision, he was *afraid*. The vision showed him that God is *holy*.

What does that mean?

What does the Bible mean when it tells us that God is *holy?*

Do you remember the story of Moses—how God let Moses see *just a little* of His glory and afterwards Moses's face shone bright as the sun? That brightness was a part of God's holiness.

But God's holiness is much *more* than shining brightness. God is *pure*. God *never sins*. God always does *right*. God is *all* light and glory. He is *all* goodness. Nothing sinful can even come *near* Him—it would be burned away by His holiness.

Oh, we just cannot *think* all that God's hol-

iness means. The angels and the seraphim *see* it, and they praise Him day and night. They sing to Him, and they serve Him. The angels are holy,

too. They do not sin. But God is *much more* holy than the angels. That is why the seraphim covered their faces and their feet. That is why they call Him Lord of hosts.

If nothing sinful can go to God, how can *we* go to Him? When we think how sinful we are, and how great and holy God is, we do not *dare* go to Him. We would not even dare *pray* to Him, if we could see how holy He is.

But God *wants* us to come to Him. Oh, He is so good to us! He told Isaiah not to be afraid. And He tells *us* not to be afraid. But He also tells us, in the Bible, that we can only go to Him in *Jesus' Name. Jesus* is holy. Jesus is God, *too,* you know. But He took little children in His arms— little sinful children. He wanted to bring them to God the Father. And we can go to God *today* if we go in Jesus' Name, because Jesus *died* to take our sins away, to make us *clean,* so that even our *holy* God will let us come to Him.

SOMETHING TO TALK ABOUT:
How can sinful people go to a holy God?
Why do we pray to God in Jesus' Name?
How do I know that I am sinful?

MEMORY VERSE
Shall we learn the song of the seraphim?

Holy, holy, holy, is the Lord of hosts: the whole earth is full of his glory.

ISAIAH 6:3

SUGGESTED READING:
Psalm 99

HYMN
Holy, holy, holy! Lord God almighty!
Early in the morning our song shall rise to Thee;
Holy, holy, holy! merciful and mighty!
God in three persons, blessed Trinity!

NICAEA
(HY 116; JS 70)

A PRAYER:
O holy Lord God, Thou art so very, very great! If the angels sing and the mountains tremble, surely we ought to praise Thee too! Oh, we thank Thee that we may come to Thee in Jesus' Name, and need not be afraid. Forgive all our sins, and make us holy, too. *Amen.*

12

God Is Almighty

The kings of long ago were powerful. They ruled over the people. Everybody had to obey the king. Those who dared to disobey were punished.

King Nebuchadnezzar was a mighty king. He had many servants. He told his servants what to do, and they always obeyed him. Nebuchadnezzar had a big army, too. His soldiers were brave and strong. They went where he sent them.

Nebuchadnezzar sent his soldiers to countries all around, to make all those countries a part of his kingdom. He became a *very* great king.

Then Nebuchadnezzar built a beautiful city. He called it Babylon. It was a city of palaces and gardens. There had never been such a wonderful city before, all bright with white stones and sparkling gold.

One day King Nebuchadnezzar walked in his own beautiful palace. He was proud and happy. He looked at all the beauty of Babylon, and he said, "What a great king I am! *I* have built this beautiful city. *My* power has won me this great kingdom."

But all of a sudden he heard a voice from heaven. The voice said, "O King Nebuchadnezzar, your kingdom is *gone!* It is taken away from you. Your servants will drive you out of your palace. You will have to live out-of-doors, like an *animal*. . . ."

And that is what happened. Nebuchadnezzar, the great king, was chased away out of his palace. For a long time he lived out in the fields, like a *wild* man.

But one day, as Nebuchadnezzar walked in the field, he looked up to heaven, and he thought of God. Then he began to *praise* God. He said, "God is King above all. He does *His* will in heaven and on earth." Nebuchadnezzar knew, at last, that *he* was very small, and God is very great.

After *that*, God gave the kingdom back to Nebuchadnezzar.

Nebuchadnezzar was a great king, a mighty king. But he was very small beside *God*. God is *almighty*. God made heaven and earth; He just spoke, and it was there! And God has *all things* in His hand. He guides and rules *all* kings and kingdoms of the earth. He rules the heavens,

too. *He* is king of everything and everybody! We are just His little creatures.

Nebuchadnezzar learned this at last, and he said:

All the inhabitants of the earth are reputed as nothing.

(DANIEL 4:35)

God is so mighty and great that we are as *nothing* next to Him.

SOMETHING TO TALK ABOUT:
Who made Nebuchadnezzar a great king?
Why did God take the kingdom away from him?
Why did He give it back to him?

SUGGESTED READING:
Daniel 4:34, 35

A HYMN TO SING:
  Praise to the Lord, the Almighty, the King
    of creation!
  O my soul, praise Him, for He is thy
    health and salvation!
  All ye who hear,
  Now to His temple draw near;
  Join me in glad adoration!

LOBE DEN HERREN
(CH 188; HY 3; JS 86)

A PRAYER:
  Great and almighty God, we cannot even think how great Thou art. And we are so small! We thank Thee for Thy love, and for Thy care over us. Help us never to be proud. Help us to remember that Thou art King over all, and all that we have belongs to Thee. Then we will praise Thee forever. *Amen.*

22

God
Is Faithful

Do you ever make promises? And do you always *keep* your promises? Maybe you promised Mother that you would be good. But it's so *hard* to be good all the time. If you are *not* good, you are not keeping your promise, are you?

People *break* their promises very, very often. Sometimes they forget. Sometimes they make promises they just *cannot* keep.

God *never* breaks a promise. God never makes promises He cannot keep. And He never *forgets*. God's promises are *sure*. God is *faithful*.

The Bible tells us that God promised the Israelites, His people of long ago, that He would bring them to a new land. It was a beautiful land, with houses and farms, beautiful gardens and parks, and all kinds of good things to eat.

But the land was far away. It was far across a big, dry desert. Besides that, there were enemies—people who did not *want* the Israelites to have that land. They sent soldiers to fight against the Israelites.

It looked as if God could not keep His promise!

But God took care of His people in the desert. He gave them plenty to eat, He showed them the way, and He helped them when they had to fight. At last they were *almost* there. They could *see* the land, across the River Jordan.

But the river was *wide* and *deep*. And there was no bridge. Not everybody could swim—little babies, little lambs, and many *people* cannot swim. Oh, no! It looked as if they would *never* get there after all. There was no way to make a boat for all the people.

Then Joshua, their leader, said to the people, "Get ready to go across the river. God will keep His promise in a wonderful way."

In the morning they were ready. Joshua told the priests to go first. They carried the Ark. The Ark was a beautiful box all covered with gold. It was a sign of God's presence with His people.

The priests started out. Soon they were down to the water. They stepped *into* the water, and all at once the river *stopped*. The water ran *away* on one side of the priests. On the *other* side, far up the river, it piled up high. God did not let it run down to where the priests stood. And soon the ground under the feet of the priests was *dry*. There was a dry *path* right where the river had been.

23

The priests walked on down the path. Halfway across the river, they stood still. They let all the people walk past them. When the people were on the other side, the priests went too, last of all.

So God took *all* His people across the river. And then what happened? The people turned around to look, and they saw the water come tumbling down! The river was wide and deep again! God *had* kept His promise! He *had* brought them to the new land, with its farms and parks and gardens. He took that land away from the wicked people who lived there, to give it to the people who loved Him.

SOMETHING TO TALK ABOUT:
Was it hard for God to keep His promise to His people?
What are some of His promises to us?
What does it mean to be "faithful"?

MEMORY VERSE
God *always* keeps His promises, even when we may think He cannot:

He is faithful that promised.

HEBREWS 10:23

SUGGESTED READING:
Joshua 21:43–45

HYMN
This hymn reminds us not to be afraid, because God is faithful:

O God, thou faithful God,
Thou fountain ever flowing,
Without whom nothing is,
All perfect gifts bestowing,
Grant me a healthy frame,
And give me, Lord, within,
A conscience free from blame,
A soul unhurt by sin.

O GOTT, DU FROMMER GOTT
(HY 132)

A PRAYER:
Father, it is good to know that Thou art faithful and almighty, always keeping Thy promises. And Thy promises to us are so wonderful! *Amen.*

14
God Has Many Names

Every boy and every girl has a name. I have a name. You have a name.

If somebody asks, "Who are you?" you tell him or her your name. Your name tells who you *are*.

Mother uses your name when she calls you,

and when she talks to you, and when she talks about you. Your name means *you*. If Mother calls Tommy's name, Mary does not have to answer. If Mother calls Mary's name, Tommy does not have to answer.

God's name tells us who *God* is.

24

But God has many names. Sometimes we call Him "Father in heaven." Sometimes we say, "Mighty One." When we pray, we sometimes say, "Dear Jesus," or, "Dear Lord."

The Bible tells us about one *very* wonderful name of God.

Long ago, God talked to a man named Moses. Moses wanted to help his people because they were in trouble in Egypt. But Pharaoh, the king of Egypt, was so angry at Moses that Moses had to run away. Then, one day, when Moses was taking care of sheep, he saw a bush on fire. The bush burned and burned, but it did not burn up. Moses went to see why the bush did not burn up. And then *God* spoke to Moses *out* of the burning bush.

God told Moses to go to Egypt, to help His people. He said to Moses, "Go and bring My people out of Egypt."

But Moses was *afraid* to go back to Egypt. He was afraid of Pharaoh. He said, "What shall I tell them if they ask who sent me?"

God said to Moses, "Tell them *I AM* has sent you." God said, "My name is *I AM*."

Isn't that a strange name for God?

It is a name that tells us wonderful truths about God. *I AM* means: "I never had a beginning; I have always been; I do not change; I will always be the same." The name *I AM* tells us that God is *eternal,* that He is *forever the same,* and that He is *faithful,* never changing, always keeping His promises.

The *most* wonderful name of God is *Jesus.* It is a Name above *all other* names. The Bible says that some day every knee will bow at the Name of Jesus. *That* Name tells us He is our *Saviour.*

God's law tells us that we must use God's names carefully. We must use His names only when we *talk* to Him, or when we talk *about* Him. God's names are *holy,* because *God* is holy.

SOMETHING TO TALK ABOUT:
Why was Moses afraid to go and help God's people?
How did God's name help him not to be afraid?
Why is Jesus' Name the best name of all?

THE PROPHET DANIEL ONCE SAID:
Blessed be the name of God for ever and ever.
DANIEL 2:20

SUGGESTED READING:
Exodus 3:1–4; 10–14

HYMN
Here is a hymn to sing in praise of God's name:
Come, Thou Almighty King,
Help us Thy name to sing,
Help us to praise.
Father, all glorious,
O'er all victorious,
Come, and reign over us,
Ancient of days.

ITALIAN HYMN
(HY 117; JS 133)

PRAYER
(When we pray to God, we call to Him and He hears us. Shall we pray to Him now?)

O God, our Father in heaven, we are so glad that we can call Thee by name. We know Thou wilt hear us. Bless us, dear Lord; and help us to honor Thy holy name. *Amen.*

MEMORY VERSES OF PART TWO

The Lord he is God in heaven above, and upon the earth beneath.
DEUTERONOMY 4:39

Do not I fill heaven and earth? saith the Lord.
JEREMIAH 23:24

Thou knowest my downsitting and mine uprising.
PSALM 139:2

Great is the Lord, and greatly to be praised.
PSALM 145:3

Holy, holy, holy, is the Lord of hosts:
the whole earth is full of his glory.
ISAIAH 6:3

All the inhabitants of the earth are reputed as nothing.
DANIEL 4:35

He is faithful that promised.
HEBREWS 10:23

Blessed be the name of God for ever and ever.
DANIEL 2:20

PART THREE

All
That God Does
Is Good

God Made All Things Good

Did you see something very wonderful today?

If you really looked around, you *must* have seen something wonderful. There are many, many wonderful things all around us. The big round world that we live on is wonderful. The big blue sky over our heads is wonderful.

Sometimes white clouds sail in the blue sky, like pretty ships. The clouds are wonderful, too. They are made of tiny drops of water that sail in the wind.

At night the beautiful stars sparkle high above us—thousands and thousands of them.

There are beautiful flowers and trees. There are pretty butterflies. There are all kinds of ants that build anthills or make homes deep under the ground. There are furry animals that live in the woods, rabbits and squirrels and chipmunks. There are birds that sing and fly and make wonderful nests.

Oh, the world is a *wonderful* place!

Where did the world, and all these wonderful things, come from?

We know where they came from. We have learned from the Bible that *God made all things.* He made them long ago, "in the beginning."

Before that beginning, long ago, there was no sky. There was no big round world. There were no clouds, no trees, no birds, no flowers. There were no people.

But *God* was there. He is the *I AM,* you know. He has *always* been. And one day He began to make the wonderful things we see.

First God made the heaven and the earth, the sky that is above us and the big round world we live on.

But the sky was dark. The world was all dark, too.

Then God said, *"Let there be light!"* And there *was* light.

God *is* light. He made light in the world so that we could know *Him,* and so that we could see and enjoy the beautiful things He was going to make.

He made the oceans and lakes and rivers. He sent some of the water up in the sky, to be clouds.

He made mountains and hills. He made trees and grass and flowers. He made little birds and big elephants. He just spoke a word, and there they were!

And *everything* He made was *very good.* God is very great!

SOMETHING TO TALK ABOUT:
Where do we learn who made everything?

29

How could He make things, with nothing to make them of?

THE VERY FIRST VERSE OF THE BIBLE SAYS:

In the beginning God created the heaven and the earth.

GENESIS 1:1

SUGGESTED READING:
Genesis 1:20–25

A HYMN TO SING:
Each little flower that opens,
Each little bird that sings—
He made their glowing colors,
He made their tiny wings.

All things bright and beautiful,
All creatures great and small,
All things wise and wonderful—
The Lord God made them all.

ROYAL OAK
(CH 10)

PRAYER
(Now shall we pray together to that great God?)

O God, our Father in heaven, we thank Thee for making all things good and beautiful. And we thank Thee for the book that tells us how Thou didst make all things just by speaking the word. *Amen.*

16

God Made Us Good

There are many, many people on the earth. There are men and women, boys and girls. There are "red and yellow, black and white" people. Where did they all come from?

God made them all.

Away back in the beginning, after God had made the beautiful earth, God made *one* man. He made that man out of the ground. He gave him a wonderful body, with arms and legs. He gave him a wonderful head, with eyes and ears and a mouth and nose. He gave him a heart that beats, and a mind so he could think. Then God *breathed* into the man, and made him a *living soul.* God gave man a soul that will live *forever.* So He made man like *Himself.* Man was very different from the animals.

God called that man Adam.

God made one *woman,* too. He put Adam to sleep. When Adam was in a deep sleep, God took a rib out of his side and made a woman of it.

When Adam awoke, God gave him this beautiful young woman to be his wife. Adam gave her a name. He called her *Eve.* Adam loved Eve. So there were two happy people on earth— people without any sin at all. They lived in a beautiful garden, with trees and flowers and tame animals. Oh, everything was wonderful, and *very* good.

God made Adam and Eve so that they could have *children.* He *wanted* them to have children. He wanted the earth to be filled with people to love Him and praise Him.

After a while Adam and Eve *did* have children. The very first baby that was born was a boy. Adam and Eve were very happy with this wonderful baby. They named him Cain.

Adam and Eve had many more children, both boys and girls.

The boys and girls grew up. Then they married, and *they* had children. Soon there were many people on the earth.

God made *all* the babies that have ever been born. All the people on earth today are children of Adam and Eve. Adam was our first father; Eve was our first mother.

We know all this because the *Bible* tells us.

Man is the *most wonderful* of all the creatures God made, because He made man like *Himself*. He gave man a good mind, to learn and understand everything on earth. Man can even know *God*. God made the first man and the first woman pure, so that there was no sin in their hearts. And God made man *ruler* over the plants and animals. He made man the *highest* of all creatures.

SOMETHING TO TALK ABOUT:

Do you remember out of what God made Adam?
How did God give Adam a living soul?
How is man different from animals?

THE BIBLE SAYS:

God created man in his own image.

GENESIS 1:27

SUGGESTED READING:
Genesis 1:26–28; 2:7,8

HERE IS A HYMN TO SING:

I sing the mighty power of God,
That made the mountains rise,
That spread the flowing seas abroad
And built the lofty skies.
I sing the wisdom that ordained
The sun to rule the day;
The moon shines full at His command,
And all the stars obey.

KINGSFOLD
(HY 44)

PRAYER
(Now shall we pray to our great Creator?)

Father in heaven, we belong to Thee, because Thou hast made us. We thank Thee, great Creator, for our bodies, so wonderfully made; and for our hearts and minds that can know Thee; and for our souls that will live forever. O help us to live for Thee! *Amen.*

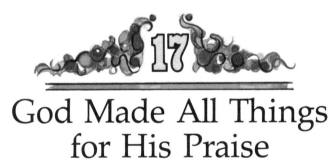

God Made All Things for His Praise

*W*hy did God make us?

God did *not* make us because He was lonely. God is never lonely.

God made us because He wanted to. He made us for His *praise*. He made the beautiful earth for people to live in—people who would be *like Him*. He wanted them to be happy and to *praise* Him because He is very great and very good.

God's work of creation was wonderful.

Everything He made was beautiful and good. *All* His works praised Him in the beginning.

How did everything praise God?

The things God made praised Him by *showing* how great He is, and by *telling* how great He is, and by being happy and good.

The stars praise God when they shine and twinkle in the sky at night. *He* holds them up there! They *show* how great He is.

The sun and moon tell us that He is a God of brightness and glory, high and holy.

The birds sing about Him. They tell us that He is a God of joy and happiness. They care for

their young, and so they show us how *He* cares for *us*.

The wind blows hard, and the waves of the big ocean splash high. They tell us that God is *strong* and *powerful*.

The trees and the flowers, the butterflies and the ants, the big giraffe and the fierce lion, the pattering raindrops and the soft white snow-flakes—*all* of these show us how *wonderful* God is. So they all praise Him. That is why God *made* them all, so that they would *praise* Him.

We praise God when we see all that He has made and say, "What a great God He is!" We say to Him, "How great Thou art!" We can praise Him much better than the animals and the flowers and the stars can. We can *know* Him and *love* Him. We look at all the things He has made, and our hearts sing: "How great Thou art!"

We praise God when we *sing songs* to Him.

We praise Him when we *thank* Him for all the good things He has made for us, and when we are *happy* with His good gifts.

We praise Him when we *pray* to Him, when we *tell* Him that we love Him, and that we need Him.

We praise Him when we *obey* Him and try to do His will.

We can never, *never* praise Him enough. He is *so* great and good.

SOMETHING TO TALK ABOUT:

How do the birds praise God?
How do the flowers praise Him?
Why can we praise Him best?

THE BIBLE CALLS EVERYTHING TO PRAISE GOD:

Let the heaven and earth praise him.

PSALM 69:34

SUGGESTED READING:
Psalm 150

SHALL WE SING THIS HYMN TO HIS PRAISE?

This is my Father's world;
The birds their carols raise;
The morning light, the lily white,
Declare their Maker's praise.
This is my Father's world;
He shines in all that's fair;
In the rustling grass I hear Him pass;
He speaks to me everywhere.

TERRA BEATA
(CH 12; JS 91)

WE SHOULD PRAISE HIM WITH OUR PRAYERS, TOO:

O God in heaven, all Thy works tell how great Thou art. They praise Thee. We, too, want to praise Thee. Give us happy songs in our hearts to sing unto Thee. *Amen.*

God Always Does What Is Best

We have learned that God is very great. He is *almighty*. There is *nothing* that He cannot do. *All* things are in His hand.

Sometimes people say: "If God is very great, why does He let me be sick, or sad? Why do troubles come?"

Even when we are sick, or sad, or when troubles come, we must believe that God loves us, and that He does what is best for us. *He* knows what is good for all of us, and *that* is what He does, even though it may not seem best to us.

The Bible tells us about a poor mother in Egypt who had to throw her baby into the River Nile. Wicked King Pharaoh made a law that all baby boys of the Israelites had to be thrown into the river, to drown.

The mother loved her baby boy very much. She did not *want* to throw him into the river.

Oh, that was a terrible thing to do! But she did not dare keep him. Oh, why had God let the king make such a law?

One day the baby's mother made a little basket. She wove it of reeds, very carefully, so that it was like a little boat. She made sure it would not leak. She laid her baby in the basket, and brought him to the river. Miriam, the baby's sister, went along. The mother set the basket among the reeds, so that it could not float away. She knew that the princess, the daughter of the king, would come to the river.

"Now you watch," she said to the baby's sister, "to see what the princess will do when she finds our baby in the basket."

When the princess came down to the river to bathe, she saw the basket. She sent one of her maids to get it.

The maid brought the basket to the princess. She opened it, and there she saw a fine baby boy! The baby began to cry!

The princess felt sorry for the baby. She did not throw the baby into the river, to drown. Instead, she sent Miriam to get somebody to take care of the baby. And Miriam ran to get the baby's *own* mother. Of *course!* Who could take better care of him?

Oh, how happy the mother was! Her baby was *not* drowned! And now she would not have to throw him into the river, because the *princess* said she could keep him for a while, at least for a few years.

The princess gave the baby his name—Moses.

When Moses grew up, the princess said he was *her* son. He had to live in the palace. He learned all the wisdom of the Egyptians. He was not a slave, like his brothers. He became a great and wise man.

Then *God* called Moses. God used Moses to bring the Israelites, His people, out of Egypt. Moses could be a great leader of God's people because he had gone to school in Egypt, where he had become a wise man.

So all the poor mother's troubles turned out for the best—the best for her, and for the baby, and for God's people too! God *always* does what is best.

God sometimes does things today that make us afraid, or sad, or anxious. Sometimes He lets wicked people do *terrible* things. But these things are always for the *best* for His own people. We must *believe* that. We must *trust* Him.

SOMETHING TO TALK ABOUT:

When God sends us troubles, does that mean
    He does not love us?
What must we do when He sends us troubles?
What was the name the princess gave the baby
    in the basket?

THE BIBLE SAYS:
Just and true are thy ways, thou King of saints.
                              REVELATION 15:3

SUGGESTED READING:
Matthew 27:27–31

A HYMN TO SING:
    What God ordains is always good;
    His will abideth holy.
    As He directs my life for me,
    I follow meek and lowly.
    My God indeed
    In ev'ry need
    Doth well know how to shield me;
    To Him, then, I will yield me.

                              WAS GOTT TUT
                              (HY 38; JS 140)

A PRAYER:

Dear Father in heaven, help us to believe that Thou art always good, and that what Thou doest is always best. Help us to trust Thee and to be happy in Thee, even when troubles come. *Amen.*

34

MEMORY VERSES OF PART THREE

In the beginning God created the heaven and the earth.
GENESIS 1:1

God created man in his own image.
GENESIS 1:27

Let the heaven and the earth praise him.
PSALM 69:34

Just and true are thy ways, thou King of saints.
REVELATION 15:3

PART FOUR

•

Sin
Spoiled
The World

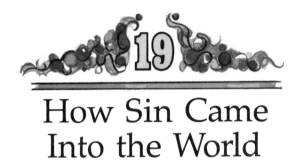

How Sin Came
Into the World

When God made the world, He made everything so beautiful and so good! And the first people were so happy! But now many things are *not* beautiful and good any more. And people are often *un*happy.

There is sickness and sadness; there is hatred and anger. There are selfish people, and wicked people. There is quarreling and fighting.

What is the matter? What has *happened* to the beautiful world, and to the people that were so happy at first?

Sin has come. Sin has *spoiled* God's wonderful world.

How did sin get into God's beautiful creation? The Bible tells us how it happened.

God has an enemy, a *great* enemy—Satan.

Satan is a wicked angel. He *hates* God. And he wants everybody else to hate God. And he tells *lies,* even about God.

Satan watched God make the beautiful earth and the starry heavens. He watched God make Adam and Eve. He saw that Adam and Eve were the most wonderful of all God's works. And he said to himself, "I will make Adam and Eve hate God, just as *I* hate God. I will spoil God's *whole* beautiful creation by making them disobey God."

Now, God had given Adam and Eve a beautiful garden to live in. There were all kinds of flowers and trees in the garden. There were birds that sang. And there were all kinds of delicious fruits to eat.

God *loved* Adam and Eve. And God wanted Adam and Eve to love Him. He wanted them to *show* Him that they loved Him. So He said to Adam and Eve, "You may eat all the fruit you like. But there is *one* tree in the garden that you must *not* eat of." By obeying God, and leaving that tree alone, they would *show* that they loved Him. God also said, "If you *do* eat of the fruit of that tree, you will surely *die!*"

Satan heard all that God said. And then *he* went to talk to Eve. He said to Eve, "You will *not* die if you eat of that tree. Instead, you will become *like God.* You will know *good* and *evil.*"

Eve listened to Satan. She *believed* him. She looked at the tree, and she thought the fruit looked very good to eat. She thought of what Satan had said—that she would be like *God* if she ate it! She forgot that she *was* like God already; God had made Adam and Eve wonderful and good, and in *His image.* Eve forgot that. She thought she would be much more wonderful if she ate that fruit.

Then she picked some fruit, and *ate* it. She ate the fruit God had told her *not* to eat. She gave some to Adam, and he ate it, too.

So Adam and Eve did what Satan wanted them to do. And they did what *they* wanted to do, instead of what *God* wanted them to do.

Adam and Eve *disobeyed* God. They became *sinners*. Instead of being like *God*, they became like *Satan*. Instead of loving God, they began to be *afraid* of Him, and even to hate Him.

Oh, that was a sad, sad day. All the happiness was gone out of the hearts of Adam and Eve. And on that day all the *unhappy* things and wicked things began.

Satan was glad. But Adam and Eve were sad. And God was sad.

SOMETHING TO TALK ABOUT:
Who is Satan?
What is sin?
Did Adam and Eve really love God?

THE BIBLE SAYS:
For sin is the transgression of the law.

I JOHN 3:4

SUGGESTED READING:
Genesis 3:1–6

A HYMN TO SING:
In Adam we have all been one,
One huge rebellious man:
We all have fled that Evening Voice
That sought us as we ran.

O Thou who, when we loved Thee not,
Didst love and save us all,
Thou great good Shepherd of mankind,
Oh, hear us when we call.

THE SAINTS' DELIGHT (SOUTHERN HARMONY)
(JS 165)

A PRAYER:
Great and holy God, we bow our heads because we are ashamed. Adam and Eve disobeyed Thee. And now we often disobey Thee! O forgive us, so that we may come to Thee again. We want to love Thee, and be happy again! *Amen.*

What Happened to Adam and Eve

Do you remember what God said to Adam and Eve about the tree in the garden? Do you remember what He said would happen if they ate of it? He said, "The day you eat of the tree of knowledge of good and evil, you shall surely *die.*"

Did Adam and Eve die that day?

Their *bodies* did not die that day. In *that* way Adam and Eve lived many years more. But they died in *another* way.

They were *separated* from God.

To be happy, we must live *with* God. It is

terrible to live without God, to be separated from God. And that is what happened to Adam and Eve.

God used to come to the garden. He would walk with Adam and Eve, and talk with them.

Right after they ate the fruit that God had told them *not* to eat, Adam and Eve were *afraid* of God. And they were *ashamed*. They ran away. They tried to hide. They tried to hide away from God; but nobody can do that!

After a while God came to the garden. He called, "Adam, where are you?"

Adam *knew* he could not hide from God. God sees *everything*. Adam came out of his hiding place. He told God he was afraid.

God said, "What did you do?"

Then Adam had to *tell* God what they had done. Oh, he was so ashamed and *so afraid!*

God is very holy. There is no sin in God. Sin makes us *un*holy. And it keeps us away from God. If we are unholy, we *cannot* live close to God.

Adam and Eve *knew* they had sinned. They had disobeyed God. That is why they were *afraid*. They knew God is holy. They knew they had to be *punished* for their sin.

God told Adam and Eve that now pain and sickness would come. He told them that after a while their bodies would die. He sent them out of the beautiful garden. They were not *fit* to live there any more. The garden was too wonderful for sinful people. He told them that now they would have to *work hard* to keep alive. And He did *not* come again to walk and talk with them, as He used to.

Many unpleasant things began on the day Adam and Eve sinned. The *worst* was this: they were *separated* from God, and *afraid* of Him.

Ever since that day, people have been afraid of God. We cannot *help* being afraid when we remember that God is very holy, and we are very sinful.

But on that same day God promised Adam and Eve that *someday* everything would be wonderful again. He promised a *Saviour*, who would take sin away and bring us back to God, so that we need *not* be afraid any more.

God still loves us very much!

SOMETHING TO TALK ABOUT:
Why were Adam and Eve afraid of God?
What did they try to do?
Can you tell in what way they died that very day?
Can you name some other unpleasant things that happened?

MEMORY VERSE
Here is a Bible verse that tells why we are sometimes afraid of God:

Your sins have hid his face from you.
ISAIAH 59:2

SUGGESTED READING:
Genesis 3:7–10

HERE IS A HYMN TO SING:
We fled Thee, and in losing Thee
We lost our brother too;
Each singly sought and claimed his own;
Each man his brother slew.

But Thy strong love, it sought us still
And sent Thine only Son
That we might hear His Shepherd's voice
And, hearing Him, be one.

THE SAINTS' DELIGHT (SOUTHERN HARMONY)
(JS 165)

(Let's ask God to help us do right):

Father, when Satan wants us to sin, help us to do what is right. We want to live close to Thee. Forgive us all our sins, for Jesus' sake. *Amen.*

What It Means to Be a Sinner

Are you naughty sometimes?

All boys and girls are naughty sometimes. Even dear little *babies* are naughty sometimes. And grownups are naughty.

Is it very bad to be naughty?

Yes, to be naughty is bad, because it is *sin*— sin against God.

Do you know what that means?

When we *sin*, we are not doing what *God* wants us to do. God made us. We belong to Him. We ought to *do* just what He *tells* us to do. We ought to *be* just what He *wants* us to be. We ought to love God, and obey Him, *always.* We ought to love *Him* because He is so wonderful, and because *He* loves *us.*

When Adam and Eve sinned against God, when they disobeyed Him and ate the fruit He told them *not* to eat, sin came and spoiled God's *whole* beautiful world. It spoiled Adam and Eve, too. Adam and Eve became *sinners.* They had let Satan into their hearts, and after that they *could* not obey God the way they should.

When Adam and Eve had children, these *children* were sinners, too. All babies are *born*

with sin in their hearts. That is why even little babies are naughty sometimes. Isn't that a sad thing?

When we do what God tells us *not* to do, that is sin.

When we do *not* do what He *wants* us to do, that is sin, too.

Oh, yes, we sin against God very much.

Many times we do not even *want* to obey God. We *want* to be naughty.

Surely, God must have stopped loving Adam and Eve when they sinned against Him? Surely He cannot love us, since we all are sinners?

Oh, God is very good and kind. He did *not* stop loving Adam and Eve. Even when He said that they would have pain and sickness and sorrow and trouble, He *loved* them.

God took care of Adam and Eve. And do you remember that He promised them something *wonderful?* He promised that someday He would send a *Saviour* who would take away sin.

God does not want boys and girls to be naughty. But He does *not* stop loving you when you are naughty. He does *not* love the naughty

41

things you do. He hates *sin*, but He loves *you*. He loves you *so* much that He sent the promised Saviour. He sent Jesus, His Son, to take *away* your sin—and mine.

Oh, we ought to love God very, very much.

We ought to love Him so much that we do not *want* to sin. He is so good to us!

SOMETHING TO TALK ABOUT:
Which people are sinners?
What was Adam and Eve's first sin?
When did we become sinners?
Has God stopped loving us now?

HERE IS A BIBLE VERSE THAT SAYS WE ARE LIKE LOST SHEEP:
All we like sheep have gone astray.
ISAIAH 53:6

SUGGESTED READING:
I John 1:8–10

HYMN:
All boys and girls like this song because it tells us that God loves us even though we are sinners:

Jesus loves me! This I know,
For the Bible tells me so.
Little ones to Him belong;
They are weak, but He is strong.

Yes, Jesus loves me!
Yes, Jesus loves me!
Yes, Jesus loves me!
The Bible tells me so.

WARNER
(CH 152)

SHALL WE PRAY TOGETHER?
Jesus, we are so glad that You love us. I am glad You love me even when I am naughty. Forgive all my naughtiness of today. Help me to love You more and more and more. *Amen.*

MEMORY VERSES OF PART FOUR

For sin is the transgression of the law.
I JOHN 3:4

Your sins have hid his face from you.
ISAIAH 59:2

All we like sheep have gone astray.
ISAIAH 53:6

PART FIVE

•

God's
Law

How God Gave Us
His Law

We have learned that God made all people. All people *belong* to God. I belong to God. You belong to God. *Everybody* belongs to God, because He made all people.

And because we belong to God, we must *live* for Him. We must live to *please* Him. We must live the way *He* wants us to live.

God has *told* us how we must live. God gave His *law*. His law tells us what we *must* do, and what we must *not* do. His law tells us what kind of people His children should be.

Long ago, when the Israelites were God's special people, God gave the *Ten Commandments*.

The Israelites were living in tents. There were rows and rows of tents around Mount Sinai.

Moses was the leader of God's people. He had led them out of Egypt. One day God said to Moses, "Tell the people to get ready. They must wash themselves and they must wash their clothes. In three days I will come down to them. I will come to the top of Mount Sinai. I will *talk* to them."

God had never come down to talk to any *other* people. This was to be a *very special* visit of God. The Israelites could hardly wait. They cleaned their tents; they washed themselves and their clothes.

Early in the morning, on the third day, the Israelites looked out of their tent doors. They wondered how God would come down to them. They looked at Mount Sinai. They saw a *big black cloud* on the top of the mountain. They heard roaring *thunder* up there. And they saw bright *lightning* flash through the dark cloud.

Moses called to the people, "Come, gather near the mountain!"

When they were all near the mountain, God came down. He came down in fire and smoke. The mountain *shook* when He came down on it. The people were afraid. Now they could *see* and *hear* that God was very great.

Then they heard God's *voice*. God said:
I am the Lord Thy God.
Thou shalt have no other Gods before me.
Thou shalt not make thee a graven image.
Thou shalt not take the name of the Lord thy
  God in vain.
Remember the sabbath day, to keep it holy.
Honor thy father and thy mother.
Thou shalt not kill.
Thou shalt not commit adultery.
Thou shalt not bear false witness.
Thou shalt not steal.
Thou shalt not covet anything that is thy
  neighbor's.

These are the Ten Commandments. God

Himself spoke these commandments from the top of the mountain. And His voice was like thunder.

All the people backed away from the mountain. They were afraid. Moses said, "Do not be afraid. God is showing you how great He is, so that you will *surely* obey Him!" And they *promised* to obey. They said, "We will do *all* that the Lord says."

SOMETHING TO TALK ABOUT:

From what mountain did God give His law?
What did the Israelites see on the mountain?
What did they hear?
Why must people do what God says?

MOSES SAID TO THE PEOPLE:

The Lord . . . is . . . a mighty God and terrible.
DEUTERONOMY 7:21

SUGGESTED READING:
Exodus 19:16–19

HERE IS A HYMN ABOUT GOD'S LAW:

Most perfect is the law of God,
Restoring those that stray;
His testimony is most sure,
Proclaiming wisdom's way.

The precepts of the Lord are right;
With joy they fill the heart;
The Lord's commandments all are pure,
And clearest light impart.

STRACATHRO
(CH 76; HY 53)

A PRAYER:

Dear Father, we will try to keep Thy law. We want to live for Thee. O help us to do right every day, in our work and in our play. *Amen.*

What the Law Means

God's law means that we must always put *God first.*

We must *love* God more than anybody else.

We must *obey* God before we obey anybody else.

We must do *all* that God wants us to do.

We must praise God every day, and in everything we do.

The Bible tells us about a poor widow woman, and how she put God first.

46

One day the poor widow went out to pick up little sticks. There was a great famine in the land. God did not let rain come, because the people were wicked. And because there was no rain, nothing would grow. There was no grain for making flour.

This poor widow had only a little flour left. She was picking up the sticks to make a fire, to bake bread with that last little bit of flour. She had only a little oil left, too, to bake with.

While she picked up the sticks, a man came down the road. He had long hair and a big beard, and his clothes were all dusty.

The man called to the widow woman, "Please, will you get me a drink?" He was hot and thirsty.

The widow woman said, "Yes, I will get you a little water."

But when she went away, the man called to her, "Bring me a little bread, too!"

Then the widow woman looked very sad. "I have no bread at all," she said. "I have just a little bit of flour, and a little bit of oil. I was going to make a fire, and bake bread for me and my son. And when that is gone, we will have to *die.*"

The man said, "Do not be afraid. Go and bake your bread. But make the first little loaf for *me,* and bring it to me. Then make some for your son and for yourself. God says that you will have flour left, and oil too. There will *always* be flour and oil left for you, until the rain comes and things grow again."

That man was God's prophet, Elijah. When the widow woman heard what he said, she went and baked her bread. And she brought the *first* little loaf to Elijah. *She* was hungry, and her *boy* was hungry, but she gave the *first* loaf to Elijah, because he was a man of God. She put *God* first. She *believed* His word, that the prophet spoke, and she *obeyed* Him.

God blessed the poor widow woman. She baked bread *every* time she and her boy and Elijah needed something to eat. And there was *always* a little flour left, and a little oil left, as God had promised.

SOMETHING TO TALK ABOUT:

What was the widow woman doing when Elijah came?
What did Elijah ask for?
How did the woman show that she loved God?

MEMORY VERSE

If we really love God, we will always try to put Him first, in everything. This verse will remind us:

Thou shalt love the Lord thy God with all thine heart.

DEUTERONOMY 6:5

SUGGESTED READING:
I Kings 17:8–16

HYMN

Here is a hymn about loving God and obeying His Law:

To those who help in Christ have found
And would in works of love abound
It shows what deeds are His delight
And should be done as good and right.

HERR JESU CHRIST,
DICH ZU UNS WEND
(HY 183; JS 74)

A PRAYER:

Help us, dear Father in heaven, to keep Thy commandments. The sin in our hearts is very strong. Help us to remember to be loving and kind, and to love Thee best of all. *Amen.*

47

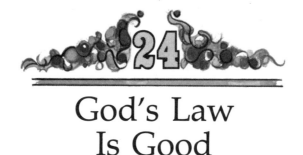

God's Law
Is Good

Are you happy when you are naughty?

Oh, no! Being naughty *never* makes children really happy.

Disobeying God's law never makes grown-ups happy, either.

To be happy, we must obey God's law. We must *love* God and know that *He* loves *us*.

God made us for Himself, you know. And we cannot be happy unless we make *Him* happy. We are happy only when we are what *He* wants us to be.

Are you happy when Mother is cross with you? No! But you *are* happy when Mother is pleased with you. And so *we* are happy when *God* is pleased with us. That is why we should obey His law.

And there is another reason. If we do *not* obey, He will *punish* us. He *must* punish us, because that is *right*.

Long ago there was a little boy named Josiah. The Bible tells us that he was a prince. Amon, his father, was king of God's people, the Israelites.

Amon was a wicked king. He did not obey God. Other kings before him had been wicked, too. They did not love God and worship Him in His Temple. Instead, they worshiped idols. And they taught *all* the people to worship idols.

One day wicked King Amon was killed. Then Josiah had to take his father's place. *He* had to be king.

Josiah was only a little boy, *eight* years old. But when they made him king, he said, "I will *not* be a wicked king. I love the Lord. I will *serve Him*."

So Josiah told the people to put away their idols. He wanted all of them to serve God.

One day Josiah sent some of his men to the Temple of God. "Repair the Temple, and clean it," he said, "so that we can serve the Lord in His own house again."

The men went to work. They found heaps of rubbish in the Temple. They found broken doors, and holes in the walls. . . .

One day a man went running to the palace, to King Josiah. "Look what I found!" he said to the king. "An old book! It was in the rubbish in the Temple!"

"Read it to me," said King Josiah.

The man opened the book and began to read. King Josiah listened. What he heard was wonderful; but it was awful, too. The book was all about God's *law*. It had been lost. It was wonderful to hear it again after it had been lost. But oh, it said awful things about what would happen if God's people worshiped idols!

King Josiah jumped up. "Oh, we have sinned against God very much!" he said. "We have disobeyed His law! We are going to be punished! Go call *all my people*, and read the book to them!"

All the people came, and they listened to God's law. They heard how God had said He

would *surely* punish them if they worshiped idols. Then they were sorry for their sins. They told God they would serve Him just as He wanted them to. The law told them how to *please* God, so that they would not need to be punished. The law helped them to be good.

SOMETHING TO TALK ABOUT:

How is God's law good for us?

MEMORY VERSE

When we do not know what God wants of us, we are in the dark. But His law is like a lamp. It shows us what we must do and how we must live. Long ago a song writer said this about God's law:

Thy word is a lamp unto my feet, and a light unto my path.

PSALM 119:105

SUGGESTED READING:

II Kings 23:1–3

HYMN

Here is a hymn about keeping God's commandments:

Oh, that the Lord would guide my ways
To keep His statutes still!
Oh, that my God would grant me grace
To know and do His will!

Make me to walk in Thy commands—
'Tis a delightful road—
Nor let my head or heart or hands
Offend against my God.

TALLIS' ORDINAL
(CH 50; HY 123)
EVAN
(CH 19; JS 141)

A PRAYER:

Father, we thank Thee for Thy law that tells us how to be happy and good. Help us to obey it just the way we should. *Amen.*

49

Why We
Disobey God's Law

It's nice to be a good girl, or a good boy, isn't it? When you are good you are happy. You can sing, you can hop and skip and play.

But when you have been naughty, everybody is sad. *Mother* is sad, *Daddy* is sad, and *you* are sad. Happiness is *all gone*.

Then why aren't you good all the time?

Well, it's *hard* to be good all the time.

Even *grown-ups* are not good all the time.

Why is it so hard to be good?

It is hard because we have *sin* in our hearts. You remember the story of Adam and Eve. Satan came to Eve and told her to disobey God. And Eve *did* disobey. She and Adam ate the fruit God had told them *not* to eat. Then sin came into the world. Sin spoiled God's beautiful world. Now *every* baby is born with sin in its heart. *Every* boy and girl has a sinful heart. And grown-ups have sinful hearts, too.

Do you remember why God made us? He made us to *love* Him, to *praise* Him, and to *live* for Him. And He tells us that we will be happy if we love and obey and praise Him.

But sin whispers naughty things in our hearts. Sin tells us to disobey. The sin in our hearts makes us cross and angry and selfish. Sin puts fun and play and other things first, and we forget to put *God* first.

God's law says we must love *Him* best of all. Our hearts say, "*Me* first."

God's law says we must love *each other*. But we do *not* love each other as we should. We are *selfish*.

It is *naughty* to be selfish.

It is naughty to be *cross*.

It is naughty to tell *lies,* and to *steal*.

It is naughty to disobey Mother and Father.

All these naughty things are *deep* down in our hearts. Naughty thoughts come from way deep down. And then we do what *we* want to do, instead of doing what *God* wants us to do, or what Father and Mother want us to do. Sin is very *strong* in our hearts. Sometimes *Satan* even whispers in our hearts, telling us to sin, just as he told Eve to sin.

It makes us *sad* to think that sin is so strong deep down in our hearts, and to think that *all* people sin against God.

SOMETHING TO TALK ABOUT:
Why should we be good?
Why aren't we good?
Who can help us, and make us good?

THE BIBLE SAYS:
There is none that doeth good, no, not one.
PSALM 53:3

What can we *do* about the sin in our hearts? There is only *one* thing we can do. We must ask God to *forgive* us, and to take all sin *out* of our hearts.

SUGGESTED READING:
Psalm 130

Why Sin Must Be Punished

Does Mother punish you sometimes? Or maybe Father? When you have been naughty, must you sit in a corner? Maybe you have to go to bed. Maybe Mother takes your toys away. Sometimes, perhaps, she *spanks* you.

Why does Mother or Father punish you?

When you are naughty, you *must* be punished. Mother punishes you because that is *right.* All naughtiness should be punished.

And there is another reason. Mother or Father punishes you to make you *good.* Punishment helps us to *stop* doing naughty things, doesn't it? So punishment is *good* for us. Punishment is good for grown-ups, too. Punishment helps us to learn how to be pleasing to God.

God is holy. Do you remember how the seraphim praised Him, singing, "Holy, holy, holy!"? God has no sin at all. He is pure and good. He wants *us* to be pure and good, too. He wants us to be like Him.

Because God is so very holy, He cannot *let* us do wrong without punishing us. If we sin against Him we deserve punishment.

When we disobey Father or Mother, we sin against *them.* But then we sin against God, *too,* because God has *told* children they must obey their parents. Sin is very, very bad.

Sin came into the world when Adam and Eve sinned. Do you remember? After that, sin grew worse and worse. Soon there were many people on earth and they were very wicked.

God was good to them. He did not punish them *at once.* He waited a *long* time. He wanted people to *turn back* to Him and serve Him again.

But one day, when God looked down from heaven, He saw only *one* family that really tried to be good and serve Him. That was Noah's family. All the other people were very wicked. They were making God's beautiful earth a wicked place.

51

Then God said, "I will destroy men off the earth. I will wipe out *all* their wickedness."

God told Noah that He was going to send a big flood to cover the whole earth with water. And He told Noah to build an ark—a big boat. It had to be like a house. It had to be three stories high, and have a door and a window.

Noah and his sons worked hard, building the ark. And they told their neighbors about the flood. But none of them believed that a flood would really come.

At last the ark was finished. Noah and his family went in, with all the animals that God wanted to save. Then God sent the flood. The water covered the whole earth. *All* the wicked people were drowned. Only those in the ark were saved.

That was a *terrible* punishment.

But the Bible says that *all* sin should be punished with a terrible punishment—your sin and my sin, too. The Bible says that all sinners who do not turn back to God will be *lost forever.*

SOMETHING TO TALK ABOUT:
Why is punishment right and good?
How will God punish sinners someday?
May we be angry when we are punished?

THE BIBLE SAYS:
The wages of sin is death.

ROMANS 6:23

But when God sent the flood, He *saved Noah!* Yes, God is very good and kind. He told Noah what to *do* to be saved. And He tells *us* what to do to be saved. We will learn about that wonderful way of salvation in our next lesson.

SUGGESTED READING:
Genesis 8:6–16

A HYMN TO SING:
There's a wideness in God's mercy
Like the wideness of the sea;
There's a kindness in His justice
Which is more than liberty.

For the love of God is broader
Than the measure of man's mind,
And the heart of the Eternal
Is most wonderfully kind.

HOLY MANNA (SOUTHERN HARMONY)
(JS 100)

A PRAYER:
Great and holy God, we know our hearts are very sinful. We deserve to be punished, like the wicked people of Noah's day. But, O God, be merciful to us; forgive us our sins, for Jesus' sake. *Amen.*

MEMORY VERSES OF PART FIVE

The Lord . . . is . . . a mighty God and terrible.
DEUTERONOMY 7:21

Thou shalt love the Lord thy God with all thine heart.
DEUTERONOMY 6:5

Thy Word is a lamp unto my feet, and a light unto my path.
PSALM 119:105

There is none that doeth good, no, not one.
PSALM 53:3

The wages of sin is death.
ROMANS 6:23

PART SIX

God Loves Us

God Gave His Son For Us

Do you remember our last lesson, about sin? We learned that *all* of us are sinners, and we all should be *punished*. God does what is *right*, and sin *must* be punished.

But God does not *want* to punish us. God— the *holy* God—*loves* us even though we are very sinful.

You remember how He saved Noah, in the ark. That is a wonderful story. God was good to Noah. But the most wonderful story in all the world is the story of how God saves *us.*

Do you know what He did to save us? He sent His *Son,* His very own Son, to *take* the punishment for us. God punished *our* sins in Jesus when He died on the cross. And now *we,* if we *believe* in Him, do not have to be punished for sin at all!

The Bible tells us how Jesus came to earth as a little baby, who was born in Bethlehem. His mother, Mary, laid Him in a manger. A manger is a box that cattle eat from.

On the hills outside of Bethlehem, some shepherds were watching their sheep that night. Suddenly they saw a very bright light. It was light from *heaven.* It was a bright angel coming down!

The shepherds were terribly frightened. But the angel told them not to be afraid. He said,

"I have *good news* for you. Unto you is born this day, in the city of David, a *Saviour,* which is Christ the Lord!"

Oh, that was wonderful news! Long, long ago God had *promised* to send a Saviour. And now the Saviour had *come!*

Then the shepherds saw a great *host* of shining angels in the sky. These angels sang, "Glory to God!" The shepherds stood there, looking up and listening to the wonderful song. Nobody had ever heard such a choir of angels before.

When the angels went back to heaven, the shepherds hurried to Bethlehem. They *saw* the Saviour there, the baby Jesus. And they were very, very happy.

Jesus lived on earth about thirty years. He did many good things. He healed the sick. He made the blind see. He went everywhere doing good.

And then—then He did the most *wonderful* thing of all. He *gave* Himself to *die* on the cross for us. He died on the cross to pay for all our sins. He took the punishment *we* should have had.

Oh, how good God is! How He *loves* us! He sent His Son, Jesus, to die for us. And oh, how *Jesus* loves us! He was *willing* to go to the cross for us.

And now God gives *eternal life* to all who believe in Jesus. We will live with Him forever and ever, to love Him and serve Him, and to be happy—*always* happy.

SOMETHING TO TALK ABOUT:
Why did the angels sing when Jesus was born?
What did Jesus come to do for us?
How much does God love us?

THE BIBLE SAYS:

The gift of God is eternal life through Jesus Christ our Lord.

ROMANS 6:23

SUGGESTED READING:
Luke 2:8–18

HYMN
Here is a hymn to sing about the coming of Jesus:

Come, Jesus, holy Child, to me;
Close tight my heart to all but Thee;
And stay close to me through all my days;
Then let me sing in Heaven Thy praise.

PUER NOBIS NASCITUR
(CH 77; HY 92; JS 4, 32)

PRAYER
(Our heart should be full of joy when we think that Jesus came to be our Saviour. Let's thank God for His great love):

Dear Father, how can we ever thank You enough for Your great gift to us at Christmas time! O Jesus, how we love You, because You died for us on the cross. Help us to be more thankful, and to sing God's praises as the angels did. *Amen.*

God Takes Care of Us

God loves us very much. He showed His great love by giving His dear Son, Jesus, to *die* for us. Surely, if He loves us so much, He will *always* take care of us, won't He?

The Bible says that He will. The Bible tells us that no matter *what* happens, He is taking care of us. Day and night, every day and all night, He watches over us.

Do you remember David, the shepherd boy who became a great king? David loved God. And David knew that God loved *him*. David wrote many Psalms or songs. Some of them are in the Bible. One of his songs is called the Shepherd Psalm.

When David was a shepherd boy, he took *good care* of his sheep. He found grass for them to eat. He led them to good clean water, so that they could drink. When the sun shone hot, he found a shady place for them, to rest. And he always *watched*. He watched to see that the little lambs did not fall off the high rocks, or get hurt in some other way. He watched to make sure that a bear or a lion did not catch one of the sheep. Before it was dark, he gathered all the sheep into the fold, the big sheep-house. There they were safe and warm. Then David lay down in the doorway, so that nothing could get in to harm the sheep at night. David was a very good shepherd. He would even give his *life* if something came to get the sheep.

When David thought how he took care of his sheep, he thought of the Lord God, how He takes care of *His* sheep. And so he wrote this Psalm, about the Lord taking care of His sheep. David knew *he* was one of the Lord's sheep. And he knew the Lord was a *good* Shepherd.

One day Jesus said to His disciples, "I am the good shepherd."

Yes, the Lord Jesus is a *very* good shepherd, a very special shepherd. He watches over us all the time, and He never even goes to sleep!

And who are Jesus' sheep? Do you *know*?

Yes, all God's people are Jesus' sheep. Jesus takes care of them, just as David took care of *his* sheep. Boys and girls are Jesus' *lambs*. He *loves* them. He watches over them, just as David watched over the lambs in *his* flock. God *loves* us. He takes *care* of us.

When we remember that He loves us, we can be happy *even* when we are sick. We can be happy in time of trouble. We can be happy when it is time for us to die and go to heaven. There we will *see* our Good Shepherd. Shall we read David's song about our Shepherd?

SUGGESTED READING:
Psalm 23

SOMETHING TO TALK ABOUT:
What does "I shall not want" mean?
What does the last line of the Psalm mean?

MEMORY VERSE
We should learn the whole Psalm someday. Perhaps we can memorize the first line today:

The Lord is my shepherd; I shall not want.

PSALM 23:1

HYMN

Here is a song we can sing to Jesus, our Shepherd:

Saviour, like a shepherd lead us;
Much we need Thy tender care.
In Thy pleasant pastures feed us;
For our use Thy folds prepare.
Blessed Jesus, Blessed Jesus,
Thou hast bought us, Thine we are.
Blessed Jesus, Blessed Jesus,
Thou hast bought us, Thine we are.

BRADBURY,
OR NETTLETON
(JS 135)

AND HERE IS A BEDTIME PRAYER TO OUR GOOD SHEPHERD:

Jesus, tender Shepherd, hear me,
Bless Thy little lamb tonight;
Through the darkness be Thou near me,
Keep me safe till morning light. *Amen.*

God Turns Our Troubles Into Good

If God loves us and takes care of us, why do troubles come? God's children get sick sometimes. They have sorrows and pains. Even God's little lambs get sick sometimes, or get hurt. When troubles come, is God *forgetting* to take care of us?

Oh, no! Troubles come for our *good*.

That seems strange, doesn't it? How can trouble be for our good?

The Bible tells a wonderful story about a boy named Joseph. He had many troubles. But all his troubles turned out for his good, and for the good of many more of God's people, too.

Joseph had ten older brothers. They were not always good boys. Sometimes they did things that were wrong. Joseph was a *good* boy. Yes, there was sin in *his* heart, too. But he *tried* to do the right things. Joseph's father, Jacob, loved Joseph very much.

Sometimes Joseph told his father about the wrong things his big brothers did. That made his brothers angry. After a while they hated Joseph.

One day Jacob sent Joseph to see how his brothers were getting along. They were far from home. They had gone away to find better pasture for their sheep. Joseph went to find them.

The brothers saw Joseph come. They said to each other, "Let's get rid of Joseph!"

So, when Joseph came near, they grabbed hold of him. They threw him down into a deep dark hole. Joseph cried. He said, "Please let me out! Let me go home!" But the brothers would not listen.

After a while some men came by, riding on camels. Joseph's brothers said, "Let's *sell* Joseph to these men. They will take him far away. Then we will *never* see him again. We will be rid of him, and we will tell our father that a wild animal killed him."

They *did* sell Joseph. And they told their father, Jacob, that a wild animal had killed him. But the men took Joseph to Egypt. He became a slave in Egypt.

Years went by. Then came a famine. There was hardly anything to eat. There was no rain. The grain did not grow. Joseph's brothers did not have bread for their families.

One day Jacob said to his sons, "I have heard that there is bread in Egypt. Go there and buy some." So the brothers went.

In Egypt they talked to a great man, who was next to the king. This man spoke angrily to them. He said they were thieves and spies. He even put one of them in prison.

The brothers said, "This is because we sold Joseph! God is punishing us." They were afraid.

But this great man *was* Joseph, and at last he *told* them that he was Joseph, their own brother. How surprised they were!

Joseph said, "Do not be afraid. I will not punish you. You did evil, but God turned it to good, so that there would be plenty of grain for all of us in this time of famine."

All Joseph's troubles turned out for *his* good and for the good of God's *people*. We must believe that all *our* troubles are for our good, because God loves us. He does not let anything happen to us that is not good for us.

SOMETHING TO TALK ABOUT:
Can you tell more of the story of Joseph?
Should we complain when we are sick or sad?
All troubles work for our good if . . . if what?

THE BIBLE SAYS:
We know that all things work together for good to them that love God.

ROMANS 8:28

SUGGESTED READING:
Genesis 45:1–8

HYMN
Here is a hymn to sing in time of trouble:

We cannot tell what gladness
May be our lot today,
What sorrow or temptation
May meet us on our way.

But this we know most surely,
That, through all good or ill,
God's grace can always help us
To do His holy will.

BULSTRODE
(CH 56)

A PRAYER:
Dear Father, help us always to think of Thy great love. Then we will praise Thee even in sickness and trouble. *Amen.*

61

God's Angels
Watch Over Us

Every great king has servants. The servants do whatever their kings tells them to do. They go wherever the king tells them to go.

God is the great King over all. He is King over the *whole* earth, and over the heavens, too. And He has a *great host* of servants. God's servants are the wonderful holy *angels*.

God *made* the angels, long ago, before He made Adam and Eve. They are His servants, and they are happy. They praise Him, and they do whatever He tells them to do.

We never *see* angels. We *cannot* see them, because they are spirits. But we know that God sends them down to earth to watch over us and to help us. They come into our homes, into our churches, into our schools. They go *wherever* God sends them, to do what *He* wants them to do.

The Bible tells us about a brave man named Daniel. Daniel dared to pray to God even when the king of Babylon said he must *not* pray. Daniel loved God.

The king made a law that said, "For thirty days no man may pray to his God. He may only ask *me*, the king of Babylon, for what he needs. If any man prays to his God, he will be thrown to the lions."

Daniel always knelt to pray to God, *three* times every day. When Daniel heard about the new law, he went to his house and knelt down to pray just as he *always* did.

The windows of Daniel's house were open. Some men saw him kneel down to pray. They hated Daniel. They ran to tell the king that Daniel disobeyed the new law. They wanted the king to throw him to the lions.

They said, "O King, you know the new law. Nobody may pray to his God for thirty days. If anybody does pray to his God, he must be thrown into the den of lions. Well, we saw Daniel kneel down to pray!"

Then the king was sad. He liked Daniel. But he could not let *anybody* disobey his law. So he sent for Daniel. And he told his servants to throw Daniel to the lions.

Poor Daniel! When the men threw him in, he fell down, down, to the floor of the lions' den. The lions came *running* to tear him to pieces.

But . . . they didn't tear Daniel to pieces! They couldn't. They were hungry. They *wanted* to eat Daniel. But God sent an *angel* to keep them away from Daniel. They could not even open their mouths to eat him.

In the morning the king looked down into the den. He called out, "Daniel, was your God able to save you?"

Daniel answered, "My God sent his angel to shut the lions' mouths."

God sends angels to take care of His children today, too. We cannot see them, but we know they are near because the Bible says so.

SOMETHING TO TALK ABOUT:

Do you remember a story about angels praising God?
Do you think they are happy, serving God?
In what way, do you Think, are angels helping us?

THE BIBLE SAYS:
For He shall give his angels charge over thee.

PSALM 91:11

SUGGESTED READING:
Daniel 6:16–23

HYMN

It makes us happy that God and His angels watch over us. Here is a song to sing when you go to bed:

All praise to Thee, my God, this night
For all the blessings of the light.
Keep me, oh, keep me, King of kings,
Beneath Thine own almighty wings.

Oh, may my soul on Thee repose,
And with sweet sleep mine eyelids close,
Sleep that may me more vigorous make
To serve my God when I awake.

TALLIS' CANON
(CH 63; HY 179; JS 109, 188)

PRAYER:

Father we thank Thee for the angels that watch over us. Help us to be Thy servants too, happy, as the angels are, to do Thy will. *Amen.*

God Wants Us to Be Happy

Did you thank God today for the good things He gave you?

He gave you *many* good things. He gives us many blessing every day.

He gave you people to love you and take care of you. He gave us our home. He gives us food—good food, and all we need. He gives us our clothes, warm clothes, maybe even pretty clothes.

Sometimes God sends sunshine. Sometimes He sends rain. Both sunshine and rain are good gifts. The snow is His good gift, too. How pretty the snowflakes are! And what fun we have playing in the snow!

God made the birds that sing for us. He made flowers to bloom in our gardens, and in the woods, and everywhere along the roads. He made the earth beautiful, to make us happy.

God makes the sun rise every morning. Sometimes He paints the sky with beautiful colors when the sun goes down. Oh, the earth is *full* of His good gifts.

When God made Adam and Eve, He put them in a beautiful garden. There were many beautiful things in the garden to make them happy. But Adam and Eve sinned, as you know. They disobeyed God. *Then* God might have said to them, "You do not *deserve* to have beautiful things. I will take *all* the beautiful things away from you."

But God did *not* say that.

Oh, yes, He sent them out of the garden. And He told them that they would have to work hard. He said there would be weeds and thorns to bother them. He told them they would have sadness and pain. But He left *many* good and pleasant things for them, so that they could *still* be at least a little *bit* happy. Oh, God was so good to them. And God is good to *us*, too. He gives us *many* things to make us happy.

Why does God give us so many good things?

Because God *loves* us. Even though we still sin against Him every day, He loves us just the same. We *know* He loves us, because He gives us these *many* things to make us happy and to make life pleasant.

When we think of all that He gives us, we want to love *Him* very, very much. We want to thank Him and praise Him.

He *wants* us to thank Him and praise Him. He *wants* us to love Him. He is pleased and happy when we love Him.

Real happiness comes only when we try to please *Him*, loving Him most of all.

SOMETHING TO TALK ABOUT:
Why should we be happy?
What are some of God's good gifts to us today?
How can we praise Him for His goodness?

THE BIBLE SAYS:
I will be glad and rejoice in thee: I will sing praise to thy name, O thou most High.

PSALM 9:2

SUGGESTED READING:
Psalm 100

HYMN

Here is a song of praise we can sing to God:

Praise Him, praise Him, all ye little
children;
God is love, God is love.
Thank Him, thank Him, all ye little
children;
He is love, He is love.

PRAISE HIM
(CH 27)

PRAYER

Shall we thank God together for all His goodness?

We thank You, Father in heaven, first of all for Jesus, who died for us. And we thank You for all the good gifts You send every day, even when we are naughty and sinful. We will try to do Your will, to show how thankful we are. Then we can be happy. *Amen.*

MEMORY VERSES OF PART SIX

The gift of God is eternal life through Jesus Christ our Lord.
ROMANS 6:23

The Lord is my shepherd; I shall not want.
PSALM 23:1

We know that all things work together for good to them that love God.
ROMANS 8:28

For he shall give his angels charge over thee.
PSALM 91:11

I will be glad and rejoice in thee: I will sing praise to thy name, O thou
most High.
PSALM 9:2

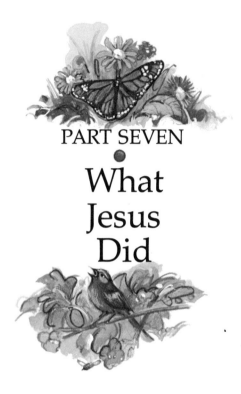

PART SEVEN

●

What
Jesus
Did

Jesus Came from Heaven

Do you know when your life began? Yes, it began when you were born. Each year you have a birthday, and then you think of the day you were born. Mother remembers that day very well. You were a tiny baby, a very *dear* little baby, then.

Jesus was born a tiny baby, too. But Jesus did not *begin* to live when He was born. Jesus lived long, long before that. Jesus is *God*, and God has *always* lived. Jesus, the Son of God, lived in heaven, with God the Father and God the Holy Spirit, long, long before the earth was made.

You remember that the earth was all good and beautiful at first. Adam and Eve were wonderful; they were made in God's likeness. But sin came and spoiled it all. God felt sorry about the sorrow and trouble that came after that. And God said, "We will send a Saviour." Jesus said, "*I* am willing to go down to earth and be the Saviour!" The Holy Spirit made a *body* for Jesus. And Jesus was born a little baby. He was born in Bethlehem.

Oh, how the angels sang that night—a great host of angels! They were so *glad* that Jesus had gone down to earth. They were glad because He went to be our *Saviour*.

What a change it was for Jesus, to come down from heaven to earth! Heaven is full of glory. There is no sickness there, nor sadness or sin. But Jesus *left* His beautiful home, and His Father, and the wonderful angels, to come down to our *sinful* earth.

Jesus was *rich* in heaven; everything was His. When He came to earth, He was *poor*. He left *all* His riches and glory behind. There was not even a house ready for Him on earth. He was born in a stable. And He did not have a *bed*. His mother, Mary, laid Him in a manger.

Jesus was *almighty* in heaven. He was Lord of heaven and earth, and Lord over the angels. When He became a baby, He could not do anything at all! Babies need a mother to take *care* of them. Jesus was *helpless*, like all other babies.

Jesus became just like us, except that He had no sin in His heart as we have when we are born.

The story of Jesus' birth is the most wonderful story in the Bible. It is the most wonderful story in all the world, and the most wonderful story in *heaven*. Just think of it—Jesus, the Son of God, became a baby!

He became a baby to be our Saviour, because *God loves* us so much and wanted to save us.

What was Jesus before He became a baby?
Why did Jesus come to earth?
What did He leave behind in heaven?

WE SHOULD LEARN THIS BIBLE VERSE ABOUT JESUS:

Though he was rich, yet for your sakes he became poor.

II CORINTHIANS 8:9

SUGGESTED READING:
John 3:16, 17

HYMN

Because the story of Jesus' birthday is so wonderful, we sing about it on Christmas day, and on other days, too. Here is a hymn to learn:

Once in royal David's city
Stood a lowly cattle shed,
Where a mother laid her Baby
In a manger for His bed.
Mary was that mother mild,
Jesus Christ her little Child.

He came down to earth from Heaven
Who is God and Lord of all,
And His shelter was a stable,
And His cradle was a stall.
With the poor, the mean, and lowly,
Lived on earth our Saviour holy.

IRBY
(CH 92)

A PRAYER:

Oh, how wonderful it was, dear Father, that day when Jesus was born! We thank You, Jesus, for coming as a little baby to be our Saviour. Help us, Holy Spirit, to love Jesus more and more. *Amen.*

Jesus
Obeyed God

Do you remember the name of the first man God made? Do you remember the name of the first woman? You know that Adam and Eve lived in a beautiful garden. Everything around them was beautiful, and they were very happy, until the day they disobeyed God.

Why did they disobey God?

God has an *enemy*. Satan is God's enemy. He hates God. Satan tempted Adam and Eve. He made them sin against God. He was *glad* when they disobeyed God.

When Jesus came to earth, Satan tried to make

Him disobey God, too. The Bible tells us how Satan *tempted* Jesus.

Satan took Jesus to a wilderness, a wild lonely place. He tried for *forty days* to make Jesus disobey God. It was hard for Jesus to say "No" to Satan all the time.

At last, one beautiful day, Satan took Jesus up on a very high hill. They could see far, all around. Satan showed Jesus all the big cities of the world, the palaces of gold and silver, the kings and princes, and the big armies.

"This is all mine," Satan said. "But I will give it all to You if You will just kneel down and worship me."

Jesus said, "Go away, Satan! The Bible says we must worship *only* the Lord our God."

Jesus *would not* do what Satan wanted. Jesus *would not* disobey God.

Jesus loved God the Father. He *obeyed* God. Every day, from morning till night, He obeyed God. He *never* did anything wrong. Even when He was a little boy, He was *never* naughty. And He obeyed God even by going to the cross to die for us.

Adam and Eve *disobeyed* God. You remember the story. They did what *they* wanted to do, not what God had *told* them to do. And we, oh, so many, many times, *we* do what *we* want to do, instead of doing God's will. But Jesus obeyed *all the time*. He said to His Father, "Not *my* will, but thine, be done."

Jesus was obedient, to make up for all our disobedience. He *had* to be obedient to be our Saviour.

And now, if we love Jesus, we will try *harder* than ever to be obedient. We will try to do *everything* God wants us to do. We *want* to do His will.

Sometimes it may be *hard* to do God's will. But He will help us. He helped Jesus, too. When Satan was gone, He sent *angels* to comfort Jesus.

SOMETHING TO TALK ABOUT:

How did Jesus show that He put God first?

Did He obey because He wanted to?

Do we really obey if we do not really want to?

THE BIBLE SAYS THIS ABOUT JESUS:

He humbled himself, and became obedient unto death.

PHILIPPIANS 2:8

SUGGESTED READING:

Matthew 4:1–11

HERE IS A HYMN TO SING:

And through all His wondrous childhood
He would honor and obey,
Love and watch the lowly maiden,
In whose gentle arms He lay:
Christian children all must be
Mild, obedient, good as He.

For He is our childhood's pattern,
Day by day like us He grew,
He was little, weak, and helpless,
Tears and smiles like us He knew:
And He feeleth for our sadness,
And He shareth in our gladness.

IRBY
(CH 92)

A PRAYER:

Dear Jesus, we thank You for being obedient for us, to make up for all our disobedience! Help us to be obedient to God, and to say "No" to Satan, and to praise You now and always.
Amen.

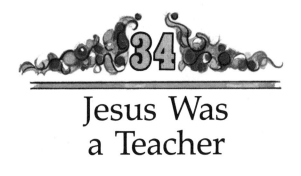

Jesus Was
a Teacher

Jesus came to be our Saviour. But He came to be our *Teacher*, too.

Jesus did not teach in a school. He taught out-of-doors. Sometimes He sat on a hill, on the grass, and He taught the people who sat around Him. Sometimes He sat in a boat, on a lake, and the people stood on shore, listening. Sometimes He stood on the porch of the Temple and talked to people who had come to worship God. And often, when He walked through the city streets or down a country road, people went with Him and He talked while He walked.

Jesus did not teach people how to read and write. He taught something much more impor-

tant than that—the most important thing in all the world—to *know God*. He told the people about God's love. He helped them to see the dreadful sin that is deep down in our hearts. He told them that He had come to die for our sin, so that we can be God's children. He told them about the punishment that will come to all who do not listen to God. And He told about the new earth that God is going to make, without *any* sin in it at all.

Oh, how the people loved to listen to Jesus! They followed Him wherever He went. Sometimes *thousands* sat on a hill while He told them about the Kingdom of Heaven.

Little children liked to listen, too. Sometimes He took them upon His knees. He put His arms around them. He loved them.

Especially the poor and sick and lonely, and those who *knew* that they were very sinful, loved to hear Jesus. They thought *nobody* loved them; but they found out that *Jesus* loved them. Jesus told them that they must give their hearts to God and not sin any more. And when they saw how much Jesus loved them, they did not *want* to sin any more.

Would you like Jesus to be *your* Teacher? He *will* be your Teacher if you read His words in the Bible. He *is* your Teacher when you read your Bible storybook. He is your Teacher when you go to Sunday school and church, because the Sunday-school teacher and the minister bring you *His words*. And they are wonderful words.

Peter was one of Jesus' disciples. He walked with Jesus every day, and listened to Him. He knew there had *never* been such a wonderful teacher before.

MEMORY VERSE
One day Peter said to Jesus:

Lord . . . thou hast the words of eternal life.
JOHN 6:68

SOMETHING TO TALK ABOUT:
Where was Jesus' school?
What did He teach about?
Why was He the most wonderful of all teachers?

SUGGESTED READING:
Matthew 5:1–8

HERE IS A HYMN ABOUT JESUS, OUR TEACHER:
Long ago within the temple
Stood a little boy one day,
And the doctors wondered greatly
At the words they heard Him say.

With the teachers there they found Him,
Though a lowly, learning youth,
But His answers as He told them
Were complete with heavenly truth.

Let us ever then be eager
To sit down at Jesus' feet,
To be learning from our Saviour,
And His lessons to repeat.
PLEADING SAVIOUR
(CH 98)

A PRAYER:
Dear Father in heaven, we thank Thee for sending Jesus to be our Teacher and to tell us wonderful words of life. Help us to listen when we hear His words, and to keep His words in our hearts so that we will not sin against Thee. *Amen.*

Jesus Controlled the Wind and the Sea

The Sea of Galilee is a big blue lake. Jesus liked to walk by the lake. His disciples walked with Him. He told them many things about God while He walked there with them.

One day, very many people came to listen to Jesus. Jesus said to Peter, "Shove your boat into the water. I will sit in the boat, and the people can listen from the shore."

The people loved to hear Jesus. They sat by the lake *all day*, listening to Him. When the sun began to go down, they went home. And Jesus was tired.

Jesus said to His disciples, "Let us go to the other side of the lake now."

The disciples got into the boat with Jesus. They put up the sail, and away they went, across the blue water. Jesus lay down on a pillow in the boat, and fell asleep. He was very tired.

The other side of the lake was a long way off. The sun went down. Night came. And the disciples were still sailing the boat.

And then—the wind began to blow *hard*. It began to make big waves that splashed into the boat. The disciples had to take the sail down. They were afraid the boat would tip over. They

began to row, but they could not row very well because the waves were so big. And Jesus—He was still sleeping!

The disciples tried very hard to row to shore. But they could not get there. And the boat was almost full of water. The disciples thought they would surely be drowned.

"We must waken Jesus!" they said. And they began to call Him. "Master! Master! Wake up! Don't You care at *all* that we are all going to be drowned?"

Jesus opened His eyes. He sat up and saw the wild waves. He felt the wind blowing in His face. And He saw that the boat was almost full of water.

But *He* was not afraid.

He stood right up in the boat. He began to

talk to the wind and to the waves. He said, "Peace, be still!"

At *once* the wind stopped blowing! And the waves stopped splashing!

Oh, the disciples were so surprised! They said to each other, "What kind of man *is* this? Even the wind and the sea obey Him!"

Nobody else could make the wind stop blowing and the waves stop splashing!

SOMETHING TO TALK ABOUT:

Do the winds and the waters obey Jesus today? Why does everything obey Him?

MEMORY VERSE

Perhaps we can learn the very words that the disciples said:

Even the wind and the sea obey him.

MARK 4:41

SUGGESTED READING:

Mark 4:35–41

HERE IS A HYMN ABOUT JESUS AND THE STORM:

Jesus, Saviour, pilot me
Over life's tempestuous sea;
Unknown waves before me roll,
Hiding rock and treach'rous shoal.
Chart and compass come from Thee:
Jesus, Saviour, pilot me.

As a mother stills her child,
Thou canst hush the ocean wild;
Boist'rous waves obey Thy will
When Thou say'st to them, "Be still!"
Wondrous Sov'reign of the sea,
Jesus, Saviour, pilot me.

PILOT
(JS 136)

PRAYER:

Help us, dear Lord Jesus, never to be afraid. Help us to believe that we are always safe when You are near. Even the wind and the seas obey You, and You will take care of us. *Amen.*

Jesus Commanded Sickness and Death

Jesus said that He was the Son of God. He *told* people that He came from God. Then He *showed* them that He came from God by doing many wonderful works.

He showed them by making the wind and the sea to be quiet. He showed them by healing the sick. Even death obeyed Him.

A doctor can help people who are sick. He can give them medicine. But he *cannot* make them well. Only *God* can make sick people well.

75

And only *God* can make dead people alive again. *Jesus* could do that, because He *is* God.

The Bible tells us about a little girl who was very sick. Her father, Jairus, called the doctor. But the doctor's medicine did not help. They were afraid the little girl would die. Then the little girl's father went to find Jesus.

When Jairus found Jesus, he fell at His feet and said, "Oh, please come to my house *right away*. My little girl is dying!"

There were so many people around Jesus that He could not hurry. One woman was sick. She came close to Jesus and touched His robe. Jesus felt her touch His robe, and He stopped to talk to her.

Jairus had to wait. And he did not *want* to wait. His little girl was so *very* sick. He was sure she was dying. He wanted Jesus to hurry.

Then somebody came running—somebody from Jairus' house. He said, "It's *too late*. Your little girl is dead."

Oh, Jairus was so sad! If Jesus had only hurried!

But Jesus said, "Don't be afraid. Just believe." It was *not* too late—not too late for Jesus.

Jairus did not think that Jesus could make his little daughter well after she had *died*.

Now Jesus went along with Jairus. They found the little girl lying on her bed. People in the house were crying. She was dead.

But Jesus took her hand. He said, "Little girl, get up!"

And she *did* get up. She was alive again! And she was well. Jesus told her mother to give her something to eat.

Jesus is wonderful. He is *almighty*, because He is *God*.

When we are sick, we pray to Jesus. *He* can make us well.

He does not *always* make sick people well. There is a time for each one of us to die. That does not matter, though. Because if we love Him, we will go to Him when we die, to live with Him in heaven forever. He has promised that.

But He can make us well if that is His will. He has power—even over sickness and death.

Jesus did many other miracles, as you know. He wanted to show people that God had sent Him. He wanted people to believe in Him and to praise God.

SOMETHING TO TALK ABOUT:

Why doesn't Jesus always make His children well?

Do you think Jesus likes to take His children home to heaven?

Can you tell about other miracles Jesus did?

MEMORY VERSE

Many people who saw His miracles were glad and did praise God. Some said:

"God hath visited His people."

LUKE 7:16

Were the people right in what they said about God? Was God visiting His people?

SUGGESTED READING:
Luke 8:49–56

Here is a hymn to sing about Jesus's power, even over sickness:

All hail the power of Jesus' name!
Let angels prostrate fall;
Bring forth the royal diadem,
And crown Him Lord of all!
Bring forth the royal diadem,
And crown Him Lord of all!

CORONATION
(HY 97; JS 88)

PRAYER:

Dear Lord Jesus, we read about the many wonderful miracles You did when You were on earth, and we believe that God the Father sent You. He sent You to be our Savior. So we praise and thank You. And we want to trust You forever. *Amen.*

Jesus
Forgave Sins

Jesus did many wonderful works. He made the stormy wind stop blowing. He healed many sick. He even made some who had died to *live* again.

Then He did something else that was even *more* wonderful. Listen to this story.

One day Jesus was in the house of a friend. Many people came to see Him. They wanted to hear what He had to say. Even great doctors and lawyers came. The house was so full of people that there was no room left for even one more.

Everybody listened to Jesus. But what was that noise they heard? It came from up above their heads. They looked up to see what it was. And there they saw four men looking down through a hole in the ceiling.

"Look out!" the men said.

They had a mat, with ropes tied to the cor-

ners. And they began to let the mat down right in front of Jesus. Down, down, down it came. The people squeezed out of the way. A *man* was lying on the mat!

"We could not get in through the door," one of the four men said, "so we took a part of the ceiling away, to get this sick man to Jesus."

They thought Jesus would *surely* heal the sick man.

But Jesus looked at the sick man, and *He* saw something that *nobody else* could see. He saw that the man's heart was sad because of sin.

Then Jesus said, "Son, your sins are forgiven."

Oh, how surprised the people were! The doctors and the lawyers were the most surprised of all. They thought, "Jesus should not say that.

Jesus is just a *man*. Only *God* can forgive sins."

They did not believe that Jesus is the Son of God.

Jesus knew what they were thinking. He said, "I will show you that the Son of man can forgive sins." Then He said to the sick man, "Arise, take up your bed, and go home."

The sick man did *just that*. He got up. He did not feel one bit sick any more. He rolled up his little mattress bed, and he went home, singing. He was so happy because he was well, and especially because his sins were forgiven. And *everybody* praised God, because Jesus did such wonderful things.

Because Jesus is the Son of God, He *can* forgive our sins. If we tell Him we are sorry, and *ask* Him to forgive us, He *will* forgive all our sins. That will make us happy. We can be happy even if we are *sick*, if we know that our sins are forgiven. Because then we know God *loves* us.

Forgiving our sins is *much* more important than making us well. It is even more important than making somebody *alive* after he was dead.

SOMETHING TO TALK ABOUT:
What did the four men expect Jesus to do?
How did Jesus surprise them?

How can *we* go to Jesus to ask Him to forgive our sins?

THE BIBLE SAYS:
Blessed is he whose transgression is forgiven, whose sin is covered.
PSALM 32:1

"Blessed" means "happy."

SUGGESTED READING:
Mark 2:1–12

HYMN
Lord, teach this little child to pray,
And now accept my prayer;
Thou hearest every word I say,
For Thou art everywhere.
Teach me to do whate'er is right,
And when I sin, forgive;
And make it still my chief delight
To love Thee while I live.
BELMONT
(CH 54)

A PRAYER:
We are glad that we can come to You, Lord Jesus, in prayer. Everybody ought to love You, because You are so good and loving to forgive us all our sins. Help us to love You more and more. *Amen.*

Jesus Showed Who He Was

Do you remember what Jesus' disciples said when He made the stormy wind stop blowing, and the big waves stop splashing? They said, "What kind of man *is* this?"

Jesus did many other wonderful works, so that *many* people said, "What kind of man *is* this?" *Never* was there another man who did all the wonders that Jesus did—healing the sick, making the blind see, raising the dead to life, and even forgiving sins!

People said, "How can Jesus *do* such things? Who *is* He?"

Jesus had twelve disciples, who walked with Him every day. They listened to Him as He told them about God.

One day when Jesus was alone with His disciples He said, "What do people *say* about Me? Who do they think I am?"

The disciples said, "Some think You are John the Baptist who has come back to life again after he died. Some say You are Elias, the great prophet of long ago. Others say You are another prophet."

Then Jesus said, "And what do *you* say? Who am I?"

Simon Peter answered quickly. He said, "You are the Christ, the Son of the living God!"

Peter *knew*.

How did Peter know?

Peter had *seen*, with his own eyes, the wonderful things Jesus did. He knew that only the Son of God could do such great works.

And Peter had *listened*, with his own ears, to all that Jesus told them about God. Only the Son of God could know so much about God and about the Kingdom of Heaven.

Best of all, Peter knew because the *Holy Spirit* told him. The Holy Spirit, speaking to Peter's heart, *told* him that Jesus was the Christ, the Son of God.

How can *we* know who Jesus is?

What Jesus did, and what He said, *shows* us who He is. We can read all about this in the *Bible*.

And if we *believe* the Bible, the Holy Spirit will speak to *our* hearts, to tell us that Jesus is the Son of God. Then we will be *sure* that He is our Saviour.

Peter and the other disciples *saw* the works that Jesus did, and they *heard* the wonderful words He spoke. We cannot see Him. We cannot hear Him. But we can read all about Him in the Bible; and we can believe. And we can be *just* as happy as the disciples who saw Jesus every day.

SOMETHING TO TALK ABOUT:

How can we find out who Jesus is?

How did Simon Peter know?

Why should it make us happy to know that He is God's Son?

79

Jesus Showed His Glory

We have learned that Jesus came from heaven. He lived in heaven long, *long* before He came down to earth as a baby.

Heaven is a place of *glory*. Heaven is all bright and pure and happy. Jesus, God's Son, was all glorious in heaven. When He came to earth, He left all His glory behind. He looked just like other men. Nobody could *see* that He was the Son of God.

But one day Jesus *showed* His glory, the glory of heaven, to three of His disciples.

On that day Jesus said to Peter and James and John, "Come with Me." And He took them up a high mountain.

Up on the mountain, Jesus knelt down to pray. The disciples did too.

Then something strange happened. Jesus' *face* began to *shine*, bright as the sun. His *clothes* began to shine, like pure white snow. When the disciples opened their eyes, they could hardly *look* at Him.

And then, all at once, two people were with Jesus. *They* were all shining bright, too. They were Moses and Elijah. They had come from heaven, to talk with Jesus.

Peter and James and John just watched. They had never seen such wonderful brightness before. It was *heavenly* brightness and glory.

At last Peter said to Jesus, "Master! Shall we make three little houses to live in, so we all can stay here?"

But just then a bright cloud came over them. And a voice said, "This is my beloved Son. Hear him!"

That was the voice of *God!*

The disciples were terribly frightened. They fell right down on their faces. They did not dare look again.

Then Jesus came and touched them. He said, "Don't be afraid."

The three disciples looked around. The cloud was gone. Moses and Elijah were gone. And the shining glory of Jesus was gone.

"Now let us go back down the mountain," Jesus said.

Afterward, the three disciples told the others about the glory of Jesus that they had seen on the mountain. And the story is written in the Bible. The three disciples never forgot that heavenly glory.

When Jesus comes back to earth, at the end of the world, everybody shall see Him in His wonderful glory.

SOMETHING TO TALK ABOUT:

What did Jesus leave behind in heaven when He came to earth?

How did He show the three disciples His glory?

When shall we see Jesus' glory?

Will we be afraid, when we see Him in His glory?

THE BIBLE SAYS:

The Son of man shall come in the glory of his Father with his angels.   MATTHEW 16:27

SUGGESTED READING: Matthew 17:1–8

HYMN:

'Tis good, Lord, to be here,
Thy glory fills the night;
Thy face and garments, like the sun,
Shine with unborrowed light.

'Tis good, Lord, to be here,
Thy beauty to behold
Where Moses and Elijah stand,
Thy messengers of old.

Fulfiller of the past,
Promise of things to be,
We hail Thy body glorified
And our redemption see.

POTSDAM

A PRAYER:

Dear Father in heaven, we want to be Jesus' precious jewels, to shine for Him. Help us to shine for Him today, like little candles burning in the night, so that someday we may shine in glory with Him. *Amen.*

Jesus Died for Us

Can you name all the days of the week? Sunday, Monday, Tuesday, Wednesday, Thursday, Friday, Saturday.

There is *one* Friday that is called *Good Friday*. It comes once every year, just before Easter Sunday.

On Good Friday we remember something very sad. Jesus *died* on Good Friday. He died on the cross.

Wherever Jesus went, He was always doing good. But some people *hated* Him. Do you remember who God's great enemy is? Yes, *Satan* is God's enemy. Satan *hates* God. And he tries to make *people* hate God. When Jesus was on earth, Satan worked hard to make people hate *Jesus*.

One day these people who hated Jesus took Him to Pilate, the governor. They said to Pilate, "This Jesus is a bad man. He makes trouble. He even wants to be king. We should get *rid* of Him."

Pilate said, "What bad things has He done?"

Nobody could think of even *one* bad thing Jesus had done. But they said, "He ought to die anyway. You must crucify Him!"

Pilate was afraid of these people. He *knew* that Jesus was a good man. But he let them take Jesus. He said, "You take Him and crucify Him."

And that is what they *did*.

They took Jesus to a hill called Golgotha. They nailed Him to a cross. And they set the cross up in the ground.

Jesus hung there on the cross, in the hot sun. The nails in His hands and feet hurt Him very much. After a while He died.

You can read all about this in your Bible, or in your Bible storybook. It is the story of Good Friday.

Was that sad Friday really a *good* day?

Yes, it was! It was the *very best* of all Fridays. It was a good day because Jesus died for us. He died so that *our* sins could be forgiven, and we could go to heaven and be with Him forever.

God the Father *sent* Jesus to die for us. And Jesus *gave* His life for us.

SOMETHING TO TALK ABOUT:
What day is Good Friday?
What makes it a good day?

JESUS SAID TO HIS DISCIPLES ONE DAY:
I lay down my life for the sheep.

JOHN 10:15

SUGGESTED READING:
John 19:11–18

HERE IS A HYMN ABOUT JESUS DYING ON THE CROSS:
What wondrous love is this, O my soul,
   O my soul,
What wondrous love is this, O my soul;
What wondrous love is this
That caused the Lord of bliss
To bear the dreadful curse for my soul,
   for my soul,
To bear the dreadful curse for my soul.

WONDROUS LOVE (SOUTHERN HARMONY)
(HY 83; JS 37)

A PRAYER:
Dearest Lord Jesus, we can never, never thank Thee enough for dying on the cross for us. We ought to love Thee very, very much. We ought to trust Thee and obey Thee and sing Thy praises every day. Help us to show our love to Thee by living for Thee. *Amen.*

Jesus
Lives Again

The disciples were very sad when Jesus died. He was their *very* best Friend. They had surely expected Him to be their Saviour. But now He was dead. How could He be their Saviour, if He was dead? They did not understand.

They buried Jesus in a tomb—a hole cut into the side of a big rock. They rolled a big stone in front of the tomb. Then they went home.

The enemies of Jesus said, "We will put watchmen by the grave, because the disciples might come and steal Jesus' body. Then they will say that He is alive again!"

But the disciples did not even *think* of stealing Jesus' body, or of saying He was alive. They *knew* He was dead and they were very sad.

The watchmen sat by the grave Friday night, and all day Saturday, and Saturday night. They did not like to stay by the grave all through the long dark night. They could hardly wait for morning to come, and for the sun to shine again. And so they were glad on Sunday morning when it began to get a little bit light.

But, suddenly, what was *that*? A flash of bright light! It came from the sky, but it was *not* lightning. Then watchmen saw what it was—an angel, coming down from heaven! They saw the angel go to the big stone that was in front of the tomb. They watched him roll the stone away. And then the angel sat on it! The watchmen were *so* frightened that they fell right down on

their faces. They did not *dare* look any more. After a little while they got up and *ran*. They ran away from the tomb as fast as they could go.

The garden was all quiet then. The sun peeked over the big rock. Some women came up the hill. They were friends of Jesus. They were bringing sweet spices to put in the grave.

When they saw that the stone was rolled away, they were surprised. They said, "Who has *been* here, and rolled the stone away? What has happened?"

They hurried on, to look inside the tomb. And there they saw the angel. Then *they* were frightened.

The angel said to them, "*You* need not be afraid. You are looking for Jesus. He is not here. He is risen! Come and *see* that He is not here."

The women went into the tomb and saw that it was empty. Then they ran to tell the disciples the good news: "Jesus is risen!"

Peter and John ran to the grave as fast as they could go. They did not see the angel there. But they *did* see the empty tomb. And then they knew that Jesus was risen. He was *alive!* He was their Saviour after all!

Yes, Jesus died. But He arose from the dead to live *forever!* He is the Christ, the Son of God. The angel rolled the stone away so that everybody could *see* that He was not in the tomb any more. He arose from the grave to prove that He is the Son of God.

Who saw the angel come and roll the stone away?

Why did the angel roll the stone away?

Who was afraid? And who was happy that day?

HERE IS A VERSE TO REMEMBER:

He rose again the third day according to the scriptures.

I CORINTHIANS 15:4

SUGGESTED READING:

Matthew 28:1–8

HERE IS A HYMN TO SING:

"Christ the Lord is risen today,"
Alleluia!
Sons of men and angels say;
Alleluia!
Raise your joys and triumphs high;
Alleluia!
Sing, ye heavens, and earth reply.
Alleluia!

EASTER HYMN
(CH 120: JS 47)

PRAYER:

What a wonderful Saviour You are, Lord Jesus! We are happy like the women were who saw the angel. And we will sing praises to You, our Saviour, alive in heaven today! *Amen.*

Jesus Showed Himself to His Friends

It was Sunday night—the Sunday after Good Friday. That very morning Jesus had come out of the grave.

The women had told Jesus' disciples about the empty grave and about the angel, and that the angel had said that Jesus was *alive*. Peter and John had run to see the empty tomb. But they had not seen the angel. Now most of the disciples were together in one room. They had the door locked, because they were afraid. They

84

thought Jesus' enemies might come and get them, too, after they had killed Jesus.

Suddenly Peter came in, his face beaming with joy. He said, "I saw Jesus! He *talked* to me!"

The other disciples shook their heads. They could not believe that Jesus had come out of the grave, and that He was really *alive* again. "It can't be!" they said.

Knock, Knock! Somebody was at the door. A voice called, "Let us in! We have good news!"

That was Cleopas. The disciples knew him. He was a good friend. They opened the door. Cleopas came in, with another man. And *their* faces were shining with joy.

While somebody locked the door again, Cleopas said, "We saw Jesus! He walked with us, and talked with us. He told us *why* He had to die!"

The disciples said, "Peter says he saw him, too! But how *can* He be alive again?"

And then, all at once, Jesus *Himself* was right there, in the room! He stood there, looking at them with love, and said, "Peace be unto you!"

The disciples could hardly believe their eyes and ears. Was it *really* Jesus? He showed them His hands and His feet, with the holes where the nails had been. And He showed them His side, where a soldier had stabbed Him. *Still* they could hardly believe it was really Jesus. But when He ate some fish and honey, at last they knew it was Jesus. It was their own dear Master, *alive* again.

Then Jesus told them *why* He had to die. Long, long ago God had promised to send a Saviour. He told them *He* was the Saviour. God had sent Him to die for the sins of the whole world, and to save His people so that they can live with Him forever.

Jesus did not *stay* with the disciples. He went away, and they did not see Him for a while. But He came back. He showed Himself to them now and then, for forty days. He wanted them to be *sure* that He was alive.

One time He met them by the Sea of Galilee, and had breakfast with them by the water.

Another time He came to five hundred friends. They all saw Him at the same time. Oh, how happy they were when they saw Him!

SOMETHING TO TALK ABOUT:
How did Jesus surprise the disciples that Sunday night?
How could they be sure it was Jesus?
How can we be sure it was Jesus?

MEMORY VERSE
Many, many years afterwards, Jesus came to John in a vision, and He said to John:

I am he that liveth . . . and, behold, I am alive for evermore.

REVELATION 1:18

SUGGESTED READING:
John 21:1–8

HYMN:
I know that my Redeemer lives;
What comfort this sweet sentence gives!
He lives, He lives, who once was dead;
He lives, my everliving Head.
He lives, all glory to His name!
He lives, my Jesus, still the same.
Oh, the sweet joy this sentence gives:
"I know that my Redeemer lives!"

DUKE STREET
(HY 152; JS 48)

PRAYER
(Jesus is alive *now*, and we know that He *hears* us when we pray, even though we cannot see Him. Shall we ask Him to bless us?)

Lord Jesus, we cannot see Thee. But we know that Thou art a *living* Saviour. Bless us, wonderful Lord. Forgive all our sins. Help us to be good, for Thy Name's sake. *Amen.*

Jesus Went to Heaven

Where is Jesus *now?* Why can't *we* see Him? Jesus is in *heaven.*

One day, when Jesus came to show Himself to His disciples again, He walked with them to Bethany. He led them up a hill called Mount Olivet. There He talked to His disciples.

Jesus said to them, "You must go *everywhere*, into the *whole world*, and tell people about Me. When they believe in Me, you must baptize them into the name of the Father and of the Son and of the Holy Ghost."

And then He promised something very wonderful. He said, "I will *always* be with you."

Up there, on the hill, Jesus did not sit down with His disciples as He used to. He *stood* by them. And when He finished talking, He lifted His hands to bless them.

Then, while He blessed them, Jesus began to go up—up—up. . . .

The disciples could hardly believe what they saw. He went up and up, until a cloud came. They watched Him until the cloud hid Him. And they *knew* He was gone to heaven.

The disciples told us this story. They wrote all about it in the Bible. That is how *we* know that Jesus is in heaven now. We are glad that the Holy Spirit led Matthew, Mark, Luke and John to write all these things about Jesus.

Do you think the disciples were *sad* after Jesus was gone? No, they were *not* sad. They were happy! They knew that He was *with* them,

and would *always* be with them, even though He was gone to heaven.

How can Jesus be with us down here, if He is in heaven? Can He be in two places at once? Yes, He can! You and I cannot be in two places at once. But *He* can. He can be in heaven and on earth at the same time.

Jesus in His *body* is in heaven now. We will see Him there when we go to heaven. But His *spirit* is on earth, and everywhere. We cannot *see* Jesus' spirit, but Jesus is always near us. Wherever we go, He is there. He hears us and sees us. He watches over us and takes care of us.

Besides that, Jesus looks down from heaven and controls all that happens on earth—the good and the bad. He has a plan, and when He has worked out His plan *everybody* will know that He is Lord of all and will praise Him.

SOMETHING TO TALK ABOUT:

How do we know that Jesus went to heaven? What was He doing while He went up to heaven? How can He be with us while He is in heaven? What does "Lord of All" mean?

MEMORY VERSE

Let's remember what Jesus said just before He went to heaven:

All power is given unto me in heaven and in earth.

MATTHEW 28:18

SUGGESTED READING:
Matthew 28:16–20

HYMN:

Far above in highest Heaven
Jesus reigns, our Lord and King;
He His life for us has given;
He did life eternal bring.
Sing then, children, sing with gladness;

Loud let grateful anthems ring!
Jesus is the children's Saviour,
Jesus is the children's King.

REX GLORIAE
(CH 132)

PRAYER:

Lord Jesus, Thou art so very, very great! We are happy to know that You watch over us from heaven above. We want to praise You. We want to tell others how great and good You are. And we love to think of the time when we shall see You in heaven. *Amen.*

MEMORY VERSES OF PART SEVEN

Though he was rich, yet for your sakes he became poor.
II CORINTHIANS 8:9

He humbled himself, and became obedient unto death.
PHILIPPIANS 2:8

Lord . . . thou hast the words of eternal life.
JOHN 6:68

Even the wind and the sea obey him.
MARK 4:41

God has visited His people.
LUKE 7:16

Blessed is he whose transgression is forgiven, whose sin is covered.
PSALM 32:1

Blessed are they that have not seen, and yet have believed.
JOHN 20:29

The Son of man shall come in the glory of his Father with his angels.
MATTHEW 16:27

I lay down my life for the sheep.
JOHN 10:15

He rose again the third day according to the scriptures.
I CORINTHIANS 15:4

I am he that liveth . . . and, behold, I am alive for evermore.
REVELATION 1:18

All power is given unto me, in heaven and in earth.
MATTHEW 28:18

PART EIGHT

About
The
Holy Spirit

The Holy Spirit
Has a Special Work

Do you remember the wonderful truth we learned about God—that He is *one* God in *three* Persons? The Bible tells us about God the Father, God the Son, and God the Holy Spirit.

God the *Father* made us. God the *Son* came to die for us. God the *Holy Spirit* came to give us new hearts and make us like God once more.

We cannot *see* the Holy Spirit. But He came down to earth one day, long ago. It was after Jesus went to heaven.

Jesus' disciples and friends stayed together, in a house in Jerusalem. Jesus had told them to stay in Jerusalem. "Wait there until the Father sends you the Comforter," He said.

So they waited, day after day. They did not know who the Comforter *was* or *how* the Comforter would come. They prayed, and they sang hymns, and they waited.

And then, on a Sunday morning, about nine o'clock, they heard a noise—a *loud* noise, like a wind blowing very hard. But it *wasn't* the wind. The disciples looked at each other. And then they saw little *tongues*, like flames of fire. But it *wasn't* fire. The little tongues sat on the heads of all Jesus' disciples and friends. And suddenly the Spirit of God was in them. The Holy Spirit *filled* their hearts. The little tongues were a *sign* that the Holy Spirit was there.

Then they began to praise God more than ever. They began to talk about God, how He loved us all and sent His Son Jesus to die for us.

Other people in Jerusalem had heard the noise like a wind. They came to see what had happened. And they heard Jesus' disciples talk about Him.

These people said, "Listen! These men are talking all kinds of languages! They talk languages of different people all over the world. They are telling everybody about the wonders of God!"

They asked each other, "What has happened?"

Then Peter stood up and said, "I will tell you what has happened. It is something that God promised long ago. You know how Jesus did great things, showing that He was the Son of God. But God let wicked men nail Him to the cross, and He died. Jesus did not *stay* in the grave, though! He is alive again. And He is gone to heaven. He promised to send the Holy Spirit. And now He has sent Him. What you see and hear is the work of the Holy Spirit. He has come to help us tell the wonderful story of salvation!"

This is the *special* work of the Holy Spirit. He makes men want to tell about Jesus. And when people hear how Jesus died to save them, the Holy Spirit helps them understand and believe and He gives them new hearts. And so He makes men love and praise God, as they should.

SOMETHING TO TALK ABOUT:

Who sent the Holy Spirit down to earth?

What happened when He filled the hearts of the disciples?

What is the special work of the Holy Spirit?

GOD ONCE SAID:

I will put my spirit within you.

EZEKIEL 36:27

SUGGESTED READING:

Acts 2:1–8

A HYMN TO SING:

Spirit divine, attend our prayer
And make our hearts Thy home;
Descend with all Thy gracious power;
Come, Holy Spirit, come.

GRÄFENBURG
(CH 142)

PRAYER

(Isn't is wonderful that the Holy Spirit is willing to live in *your* heart and in *mine*? Shall we ask Him to come in?)

O Holy Spirit, come and live in our hearts. We cannot be God's children unless we have Thee to give us new hearts. And then help us tell the story of Jesus to others, and help them believe and understand, too. *Amen.*

The Holy Spirit
Made the Disciples Brave

There was a time when Jesus' disciples were not very brave. That night when the soldiers came to take Jesus, all the disciples ran away. They were afraid. They thought the soldiers would get them, too. So they ran away, and left Jesus all alone with the cruel enemies.

Most of the disciples did not *dare* follow when the soldiers took Jesus to the hill and nailed Him to the cross. Even though they *loved* Him, they were afraid to go along. And when Jesus was buried, they hid in one room. They locked the door.

But do you remember what happened after the Holy Spirit came? Peter stood *right up* in front of everybody, and he told them all about Jesus. He said, "This Jesus was the Son of God! You must *believe* on Him to have your sins forgiven!" Peter was not afraid at all any more! What *made* him so brave? It was the Holy Spirit in his heart that made him brave.

But the people who crucified Jesus did not *want* Peter and the other disciples to talk about Him. They did not want them to *tell* the people that Jesus was the Saviour. So they said to the disciples, "*Stop* talking about Jesus, or we will put you in prison!"

Peter and John and the other disciples said, "We *cannot* stop talking about Him. God has told us to tell the *whole world* about Jesus. We have to obey *God*." And they kept on telling the story.

Then the enemies of Jesus were very angry. They *did* put the disciples in prison.

They said, "Tomorrow we will decide how to punish you."

The next morning the high priest sent soldiers to the prison. "Get those men and bring them to court," he said.

The soldiers hurried away. Soon they came back. But they did not bring the disciples. They said to the high priest, "The prison was empty! The doors were locked, and the watchmen were right there, but the disciples were *gone*!"

The high priest was so surprised! He did not know what had happened.

But *we* know what happened. An *angel* came in the night. He opened the door and let the disciples out of prison.

And what did the disciples do? They went *right on* telling the story of Jesus. They were not afraid at all. The Holy Spirit made them brave.

Later, some were *killed* for telling about Jesus. And ever since that time many missionaries have died for Jesus' sake. And they were not afraid.

SOMETHING TO TALK ABOUT:
Who wanted the disciples to stop talking about Jesus?
Why weren't the disciples afraid?
How did they get out of prison?
What did they do then?

HERE IS A BIBLE VERSE TO LEARN
Peter and John said to the high priest:

We ought to obey God rather than men.

ACTS 5:29

SUGGESTED READING:
Acts 5:25–29

HYMN
We are so small and weak! Sometimes we are afraid to stand up for Jesus. This hymn is a prayer for the Holy Spirit to make us strong and brave:

Spirit of God, dwell Thou within my heart;
Wean it from earth; through all its pulses move;
Stoop to my weakness, mighty as Thou art,
And make me love Thee as I ought to love.

MORECAMBE
(HY 109)

PRAYER
(Shall we ask the Holy Spirit to make us brave to tell about Jesus?)

Holy Spirit, come and live in our hearts. Make us brave and strong, to obey God, to do right, and to tell others about Jesus. *Amen.*

93

The Holy Spirit
Guided the Disciples

Do you like to make your father happy? The *best* way to make him happy is to be good, and to do what he wants you to do.

God is our Father in *heaven*. If we love Him, we want to make Him happy. We will try to do what He wants us to do.

But how can we *know* what He wants us to do? Well, we have His law, the Ten Commandments. They tell us to love God and our neighbors. But we have even more.

The Holy Spirit, living in our hearts, will tell us what He wants us to do. The Holy Spirit guides us into doing God's will. He guided Jesus' disciples, too. He will guide everybody who loves Jesus.

Philip was a deacon in the church, in Bible times. He was an evangelist, too. He told people about Jesus and the way of salvation.

One day the Holy Spirit told Philip to go far away, to a road in the country. There Philip saw a man riding in a chariot. The Holy Spirit said to Philip, "Go and talk to that man."

Philip ran up to the chariot. He walked along beside the chariot. The man was reading. Philip listened. He heard the man reading:

"He was led like a sheep . . . and like a lamb. . . ."

The man was reading the *Bible!*

Philip called to him, "Do you *understand* what you are reading?"

Then the man saw Philip. He said, "I need somebody to help me. Will you sit with me and tell me what it means?"

Philip was glad to help the man. He climbed up into the chariot. He explained that the prophet of long ago wrote about *Jesus*. *Jesus* was like a *sheep*, and like a *lamb* that was killed for a sacrifice. Jesus died for us.

Philip told the man all about Jesus. He told him that we ought to *believe* in Jesus and be baptized.

The man listened and listened. He thought it was a wonderful story. After a while they came to a place where there was water. Then the man said, "Look, there is water. May I be baptized right now?"

Philip said, "If you *believe* with *all* your heart, you may be baptized."

The man said, "I believe that Jesus is the Son of God."

Then they got down from the chariot. They went into the water, and Philip baptized the man.

As soon as the man was baptized, the Holy Spirit took Philip away.

Do you see how the Holy Spirit guided Philip? He told Philip where to go; He told him to talk to that man; He helped Philip explain the Bible; and then He took Philip away to work some other place.

The Holy Spirit is our wonderful Guide.

SOMETHING TO TALK ABOUT:

Why did the Holy Spirit send Philip to the chariot?

Why did the man in the chariot need Philip?

What was the man reading about?

JESUS SAID:

He will guide you into all truth.

JOHN 16:13

SUGGESTED READING:

Acts 8:29–39

HYMN

This hymn is a prayer, asking God to guide our lives:

Take my life and let it be
Consecrated, Lord, to Thee;
Take my moments and my days,
Let them flow in ceaseless praise.

Take my will and make it Thine,
It shall be no longer mine;
Take my heart, it is Thine own,
It shall be Thy royal throne.

PATMOS
(JS 152)

PRAYER

(Shall we ask for His guidance now, in our own words?)

Holy Spirit, guide us, so that we may know what You want us to do. Help us to hear You speaking in our hearts, for Jesus' sake. *Amen.*

The Holy Spirit Builds God's Church

Do you know what happened when Peter spoke to the people, that day when the Holy Spirit came? They listened carefully. When Peter said that Jesus, who was nailed to the cross, was the *Son of God*, they could hardly believe it.

Peter said, "God has raised Him up. We have seen Him after He arose. And now He is high in heaven, at the right hand of God. This Jesus, whom you crucified, is Christ, the Lord!"

Then the people were afraid. It made them afraid to think they had nailed God's Son to the cross! They said to Peter, "What shall we *do*?"

Peter said, "Repent, and be baptized, and your sin will be forgiven." To repent means to be sorry for sin.

That day *three thousand* people were sorry for their sin and believed in Jesus. And they were baptized. So the Church of God began to grow. At first there were just a *few* disciples. Soon there were many, many more. They were called Christians. And all this was the work of the Holy Spirit.

One day, while many Christians were praying together, the Holy Spirit spoke to their hearts. He said, "I have special work for Paul and Barnabas." Paul and Barnabas were fine Christian men.

The people prayed again, asking God to tell them just what to do. And He told them to send Paul and Barnabas away, to far countries, to tell *other* people about Jesus.

Paul and Barnabas became the first *missionaries*. They went through many lands. They went from city to city. And wherever they went, the Holy Spirit worked in the hearts of people, so that many believed. The Church grew and grew.

What does the Holy Spirit do?
How can we be missionaries?

MEMORY VERSE
We need the Holy Spirit to make us children of
God. The Bible says:

*For as many as are led by the Spirit of God,
they are the sons of God.*

ROMANS 8:14

SUGGESTED READING:
Acts 16:13–15

HYMN:
Spread, oh, spread, Thou mighty Word,
Spread the kingdom of the Lord,
Wheresoe'er His breath has giv'n
Life to beings meant for heav'n.

Tell them of the Spirit giv'n
Now to guide us up to heav'n,
Strong and holy, just and true,
Working both to will and do.

HÖCHSTER PRIESTER
(JS 118)

A PRAYER:
Holy Spirit, Thou dost build the Church by
living in the hearts of believers. Live in our
hearts; teach us how to live for God. Bless all
who tell the story of Jesus, so that many may
repent and believe, and so the Church will grow
all over the world. *Amen.*

There have been many more missionaries.
Today there are missionaries who go to every
country in the world. They tell the way of salvation. More people believe in Jesus. And the
Church keeps on growing.

It is the Holy Spirit who builds the Church
of God. He helps the missionaries to tell the
story of Jesus. And He puts faith in the hearts
of those who are to be God's children.

SOMETHING TO TALK ABOUT:
What does a missionary do to help the Church
grow?

MEMORY VERSES OF PART EIGHT

I will put my spirit within you.

EZEKIEL 36:27

We ought to obey God rather than men.

ACTS 5:29

He will guide you into all truth.

JOHN 16:13

For as many as are led by the Spirit of God, they are the sons of God.

ROMANS 8:14

PART NINE

How We Become Children Of God

We Must Confess Our Sins

God is *holy*, and very *great*, and *high* above us. *We* are *small*, and *sinful*. We are not good; we often disobey God. We go our own way.

Yet God calls us to be His children! How can we *become* His children?

Jesus once told a story about a young man who went away from home. He had a good home, but he was not happy there. He did not love his father.

One day the young man said to his father, "Give me all that will be mine after you die."

The father did not like to do that. And he did not want his boy to go away from home. But he gave him the money that was going to be his someday. And the young man went away.

He went *far* away. And he had fun. He spent his money. He made friends. They had fun together.

But after a while the money was *all gone*. Then his friends went away, too. They were not *good* friends. They only wanted to have fun.

The young man said to himself, "Now I must work. I need money to buy something to eat." He was hungry. And he did not dare to go home.

He found a farmer who said, "You may go out in the field and feed my pigs." That was not nice work. The young man was very unhappy. But nobody cared. Nobody felt sorry for him. Nobody gave him a good dinner. Oh, how he wished he was back home, with his father!

Every day he thought about his home and his father. He knew that even the servants at home had plenty to eat. But he did not *dare* to go home. He thought his father would not *want* him to come back. He thought his father would be angry, because he had been bad.

Then, one day, the young man said to himself, "Why do I stay here? I am so unhappy! I *will* go back home! And I will tell my father that I have *sinned*. I will tell him how sorry I am. Maybe he will forgive me. Maybe he will let me be one of his servants."

So the young man started for home.

But—do you know what happened?

The father had been thinking about his boy all that time. He still *loved* his boy. Every day he looked down the road, hoping to see his boy come home again. And so, while the young man was still a long way from home, the father saw him coming. He *ran* to meet his son. He threw his arms around him. He was so *glad* to see him.

The young man cried. He said, "Father, I have sinned!"

And the father *forgave* him. He loved his boy so much! He told his servants to make a big dinner to celebrate his coming home.

God is like that father. If we are sorry for our sins, He will forgive us. He is glad when we come back to Him, because He *loves* us.

How are we like the boy of the story?

Why was the father so glad to see him come back?

How can we go back to our heavenly Father?

THE BIBLE SAYS:

If we confess our sins, he is faithful and just to forgive us our sins.

I JOHN 1:9

SUGGESTED READING:

Luke 15:1–10

HERE IS A HYMN TO SING:

Today Your mercy calls us
  to wash away our sin.
However great our trespass,
  whatever we have been,
However long from mercy
  our hearts have turned away,
Your precious blood can cleanse us
  and make us pure today.

Today Your gate is open,
  and all who enter in
Shall find a Father's welcome
  and pardon for their sin.
The past shall be forgotten,
  a present joy be giv'n,
A future grace be promised,
  a glorious crown in heav'n.

ANTHES
(JS 160)

A PRAYER:

Father, help us to know that we are sinners, far away from Thee. We are too sinful to be Thy children. But oh, we are glad that Jesus told this story about the father who loved his boy so much. We thank Thee for Thy great love, which welcomes us back when we confess our sins. *Amen.*

We Must Know the Way

When a sinner wants to go back home to God, he must know the *way*.

You remember the story of the boy who ran away from home. When he was sorry, and wanted to go back home, he had to be *sure* to take the right road, didn't he? *We* have to take the right road, too, when we go back home, to our Father in heaven. If we take the *wrong* road, we will never get home. We will be lost.

Sinners who do not go back to God in the

right way are lost *forever*, and that is terrible. The Bible tells us that *Jesus* is the right way to God. He is the *only* way. Jesus told His disciples about that before He went away to heaven.

They were sitting by a long table. They had just finished supper. And it was their *last* supper with Jesus. Jesus had said to them, "I am going away."

They did not want Jesus to go away. They were sad.

Jesus said to them, "Do not be sad. I am going to My Father. And I will make a place ready there for you. You may come, too, and be with Me in My Father's house."

Thomas, one of the disciples, said, "Lord, we do not know the *way!*"

Then Jesus said, *"I am the way. . . . No man cometh unto the Father but by me."*

What did Jesus mean? How can He be the *way* to God the Father?

The disciples did not understand. They knew that Jesus was the Son of God. But they did not know how He could be the *way* to the Father. Afterward, when God the Holy Spirit helped them understand God's Word, they knew how Jesus is the way.

God's Word, the Bible, tells how God made Jesus the *way* of salvation.

Long, long ago God made a wonderful plan. It was a plan for saving sinful people.

Sin *must* be punished. All the sin against God must be punished. Because all people sin against the great and holy God, they should be punished *forever*. But God made a plan to send Jesus, His Son, to take the punishment in their place.

So God made Jesus the *way* of salvation.

We will learn more about this way of salvation in other lessons.

SOMETHING TO TALK ABOUT:
What is the wonderful plan the Bible tells about?
Why did God make such a plan to save us?
Who made Jesus "the way" of salvation?

MEMORY VERSE
Today we want to learn what Jesus said:

No man cometh unto the Father, but by me.
JOHN 14:6

He is the *only* way back to God, our Father in heaven.

SUGGESTED READING:
John 14:1–6

A HYMN TO SING:
Jesus, lead the way
Through our life's long day,
And with faithful footstep steady,
We will follow ever ready.
Guide us by the hand
To the Fatherland.

Order Thou our ways,
Saviour, all our days.
If Thou lead us through rough places,
Grant us Thy sustaining graces.
When our course is o'er,
Open heaven's door.
SEELENBRÄUTIGAM
(CH 64; HY 147; JS 144)

Father in heaven, we thank Thee for Thy Word that tells us about Jesus, the way to heaven. Help us to understand Thy Word and hide it in our hearts, so that we will surely know the way back to Thee. *Amen.*

We Must Believe
That Jesus Is Our Saviour

We have learned that to become children of God we must confess our sins. We must *know* that we are sinful. We must tell God we are sorry for our sins.

We have learned, too, that we can only go to God by way of *Jesus*. He told us that *He* is the way to the Father in heaven.

How is Jesus the way?

He is the way because He is the *only Saviour*. We must *believe* on Him.

What does it mean, to believe on Jesus as our Saviour?

It means that we must be *sure*, deep down in our hearts, that He died for *us*, and that the Father has forgiven all our sins. I must believe that He died for me. You must be sure that He died for *you*.

It means that we must be sure that Jesus is in heaven now, watching over us and loving us. It means that we must trust Him to take care of us *always*, even when we die, and that then He will take us to *heaven*.

Jesus came to earth *just* to be our Saviour. When Jesus was born, the angels in heaven sang. They were so *glad* that Jesus was going to save sinners. Even before He was born, God sent one of them down to tell Jesus' mother that Jesus was going to be the Saviour.

Mary was a young lady who lived in the little city of Nazareth. One day she suddenly saw an angel, Gabriel. And she was afraid.

The angel said to her, "Do not be afraid. God is *pleased* with you. You are going to have a baby—a baby boy. And His name shall be Jesus—that means Saviour!"

God gave Jesus that name, because God *sent* Him to be our Saviour.

Afterwards an angel went to Joseph. Joseph was Mary's husband. The angel told Joseph, too, that the baby's name must be Jesus, that is *Sav-*

iour. He talked to Joseph in a dream. He said, "Mary is going to have a baby, and you must name the baby Jesus because He shall save His people from their sins." That is what He *came* to do.

After Jesus was gone back to heaven, His disciples went everywhere to tell about Him. They said to people everywhere, "You must believe in Jesus. He came to take away our sins."

When we think how poor and sinful we are, and how holy God is, we are afraid. But if we *believe* in Jesus we need not be afraid any more. He will save us. God *forgives* all our sins for Jesus' sake. And He will wash our hearts clean, so that someday we will not sin any more. We will be pure and sinless. We will live with Jesus and with the Father in heaven.

SOMETHING TO TALK ABOUT:
What does the name "Jesus" mean?
Who gave Him that name?
Whose Saviour is He?

THE BIBLE SAYS:
Believe on the Lord Jesus Christ, and thou shalt be saved.
ACTS 16:31

SUGGESTED READING:
Acts 16:25–34

HYMN
Here is a song that tells us to go to the Father just as we are, with sinful hearts. If we believe in Jesus, God forgives all our sins:

My faith looks up to Thee,
Thou Lamb of Calvary,
Saviour divine.
Now hear me while I pray;
Take all my guilt away;
Oh, let me from this day
Be wholly Thine!

OLIVET
(JS 154)

A PRAYER:

O God, we can never thank Thee enough for the Saviour, Jesus our Lord. Holy Spirit, make us very sure, deep down in our hearts, that He is *our* Saviour, who came to earth to die for us, so that our sins could be forgiven. *Amen.*

103

We Must Be Born Again

Boys and girls like their birthdays. Your birthday is a *happy* day. You are glad to be a year older. Mother and Daddy remember how tiny you were when you were born. They were so happy that day!

But did you ever think that you must be born *again*? Jesus *said* so.

There was a man, named Nicodemus, who went to see Jesus one night. He wanted to talk to Jesus about God, and about God's Kingdom.

Jesus said to Nicodemus, "No man can see the Kingdom of God unless he is *born again*."

Nicodemus thought that was a strange thing to say. He did not understand it at all.

Nicodemus said, "I am a grown-up man. How can I be born again? Can a grown-up man become a tiny baby again?"

Jesus said, "Nobody can go into the Kingdom of God unless he is born of water and of the Spirit."

What did Jesus mean?

Let us try to understand what Jesus meant.

We have learned that we were born with sinful hearts. We need *new* hearts. We have learned that we must confess our sins. We must tell God that we are *sorry* for our sins.

We have learned, too, that we can only go to God through Jesus, because He is the *way*, the *only* way.

We have learned that we must *believe* on Jesus. We must believe that He died on the cross for us, so that we could have our sins forgiven.

But do you know that we cannot *do* any of those things? Sin is so strong in our hearts that we *cannot* become children of God unless the *Holy Spirit* does the work in our hearts.

The Holy Spirit makes us sorry for our sin. The Holy Spirit helps us to understand that Jesus is the way, the only way, back to the Father in heaven. The Holy Spirit puts *faith* in our hearts, so that we believe that Jesus is our Saviour.

When the Holy Spirit does this, He gives us a *new heart*—a heart that does not *want* to sin, a heart that *loves* God, a heart that wants to *please* God, a heart that asks, "Dear Lord in heaven, what do *You* want me to do?" And so we are *born again*. We are God's children. We belong to the Kingdom of God, when we have a new heart that the Holy Spirit gives us—a heart that chooses to do God's will.

Do you really want to please God?

SOMETHING TO TALK ABOUT:

Why do we need a new heart?
How can we get a new heart?
How can we know if we have a new heart?

MEMORY VERSE

Shall we remember what Jesus said to Nicodemus? Then we will thank the Holy Spirit for making us children of God. Jesus said:

Except a man be born again, he cannot see the kingdom of God.

JOHN 3:3

SUGGESTED READING:
John 3:1–5

HYMN

God will not turn us away if we ask Him to live in our hearts. This hymn reminds us that He *wants* us to come to Him:

Gentle Jesus, meek and mild,
Look upon a little child;
Bless me and remember me;
Saviour, let me come to Thee.

Loving Jesus, gentle Lamb,
In Thy gracious hands I am;
Make me, Saviour, what Thou art;
Live Thyself within my heart.

I shall then show forth Thy praise,
Serve Thee all my happy days;
Then the world shall always see
Christ, the holy Child, in me.

GENTLE JESUS
(CH 174)

A PRAYER:

O Holy Spirit, take our hearts and make them new. Then we will be children of God; we will belong to the wonderful Kingdom of Heaven! *Amen.*

MEMORY VERSES OF PART NINE

If we confess our sins, he is faithful and just to forgive us our sins.
I JOHN 1:9

No man cometh unto the Father, but by me.
JOHN 14:6

Believe on the Lord Jesus Christ, and thou shalt be saved.
ACTS 16:31

Except a man be born again, he cannot see the kingdom of God.
JOHN 3:3

PART TEN

How
God's Children
Live And Grow

God's Children
are New Creatures

Do you remember how happy Adam and Eve were in the Garden, before they disobeyed God? Perhaps you remember the verse we learned in another lesson: *God created man in his own image*. Adam and Eve were sinless and pure.

But they sinned against God. They disobeyed Him. And as soon as they sinned they were changed; they were *not* pure and sinless anymore. They became selfish, and hateful, and quarrelsome, and greedy—and very unhappy. Now *all of us*, deep down in our hearts, are like that. We are sinful. We are often unhappy. God can hardly see His image in us.

Jesus came so that our sins could be forgiven, so that we could be sinless and pure once more. When we believe in Jesus as our Saviour, God gives us a new heart—a heart that wants to live for Him. Jesus comes to live in that new heart, and all the bad must go out. The new heart wants you to do what is good and right.

But the bad does not go out all at once! You do not become pure and good all of a sudden, with no sin at all. The old sinful heart is still there, too, and wants you to do wrong.

A Christian must *grow*. God wants us to become like Jesus. You know how good and kind Jesus was. He was pure and holy, gentle and loving, and always did what His Father wanted

Him to do. Christians must become like that. They must grow to be better and stronger Christians. They must learn to do God's will. They must grow strong to fight against the sin that is still in their old hearts.

If Jesus lives in your heart, you are a "new creature," and you *will* become more and more like Jesus. Open your heart wide for Jesus to fill it with His love, and He will crowd out all the bad.

In the next few lessons we will talk more about growing.

SOMETHING TO TALK ABOUT:

How do we become "new creatures"?
What bad things can you see in your own heart?
Do you see bad in other people, too?
How can we get rid of the sin in our hearts?

MEMORY VERSE

The great missionary Paul once wrote to the churches:

If any man be in Christ, he is a new creature.

II CORINTHIANS 5:17

Can you tell what Paul meant?

SUGGESTED READING:
John 15:1–5

HYMN

This hymn tells us how God makes us new creatures:

I belong to Jesus;
I am not my own;
All I have and all I am
Shall be His alone.

I belong to Jesus;
What can hurt or harm
When He folds around my soul
His almighty arm?

GLENFINLAS
(CH 151)

OUR PRAYER:

Lord Jesus, please do come into my heart, and into all our hearts. Make us true and good. Then we will be happy, and we will praise You forever. *Amen.*

God's Children Love Him

One day, when Jesus was here on earth, one of His friends made a big dinner for Him. Simon of Bethany invited Jesus' very best friends—Lazarus, who loved Jesus very much; the two sisters of Lazarus, Mary and Martha; and many others, besides Jesus and His disciples.

Martha helped get the dinner on the table. She was *glad* to do that for Jesus. She loved Him so!

Mary loved Jesus, too. She thought of a different way to show her love to Jesus. She took a bottle of very precious perfume along from home. It was wonderful ointment-perfume that was worth a great deal of money. She wanted to give that precious perfume to Jesus.

When all the guests were sitting at the table, Mary walked around the table until she was behind Jesus. Then she broke the bottle open, and she began to pour the perfume on Him. She poured some on Jesus' head, and some on His feet. She *emptied* the bottle for Him. She loved Him that much!

The sweetness of the perfume filled the room. And Mary knelt down by Jesus, to wipe His feet with her beautiful long hair.

Some of the guests thought Mary wasted the perfume, pouring it out on Jesus that way. But she *didn't*. It was her *love* gift to Jesus. It was the most *precious* thing she had to give Him. And Jesus was pleased.

Lazarus loved Jesus, too. Mary and Martha and Lazarus were very dear friends of Jesus. Do you know *why* they loved Jesus so much?

Jesus had been in their house many, many times. They knew how very good and loving and kind He was. They had listened to His wonderful words. They *believed* that He was the Saviour, sent from God; they believed that He would take away their sins, although they did not yet know that He was going to *die* for them. They *did* know that He loved *them* very much. And so they loved *Him*.

We know that He loved us so much that He died on the cross for us. How we ought to love Him! We know that He loves us *now*, and watches over us *every minute*. If we *really* are God's children, if we really have *new hearts*, we *will* love Him, we *must* love Him—more and more.

SOMETHING TO TALK ABOUT:

What has Jesus done for you?

What does He do for us every day?

What can we give or do to show Jesus that we love Him?

THE BIBLE SAYS:

We love him, because he first loved us.

I JOHN 4:19

SUGGESTED READING:

John 12:1–3

HERE IS A HYMN TO SING ABOUT LOVING JESUS:

Jesus, Jesus, only Jesus
Can my heartfelt longing still,
Lo, I pledge myself to Jesus
What He wills alone to will.
For my heart, which He hath filled,
Ever cries, Lord, as Thou wilt.

JESUS, JESUS, NICHTS ALS JESUS
(CH 30; JS 145)

A PRAYER:

Dear Jesus, when we think how much Thou hast loved us, we want to love Thee with all our heart. We want to give Thee the very best we have, and all we have. Father, we thank Thee for sending Thy Son to be our Saviour. O God, we can never thank Thee or love Thee enough. *Amen.*

God's Children
Love One Another

Whenyou are playing a game, do you ever say, "Me first!"?

You know that is not nice to say.

Why is that not nice to say? Because when you say, "Me first!" you are being *selfish*. You are loving *yourself* best.

Is it naughty to be selfish? And to love myself best?

111

Oh, yes! God says we must love *Him* best. And God says we must love *other people* just as much as we love *ourselves*. The *sin* in our hearts makes us love ourselves more than we love anyone else.

Everybody has selfishness in his or her heart. Even Jesus' disciples were selfish. One day they asked Jesus, "Who is going to be *first* in the Kingdom of Heaven?" And each one wanted Jesus to say that *he* would be first.

Jesus had to *teach* His disciples not to be selfish. One day He gave them a lesson they would not forget.

It was suppertime—the last supper Jesus was to have with His disciples. It was a feast supper. When Jesus and His disciples came, supper was ready. They all had dusty feet, because they wore only sandals. They thought there would be a servant to wash their feet. But when they looked around, they saw a jug of water and a towel, but no servant. The *disciples* did not want to do the work of a servant. Not *one* of them would do *that*. So they all sat down at the table with dusty feet.

Then *Jesus* stood up. *He* poured water into a basin and began to wash the disciples' feet. That made them all feel guilty and ashamed. Think of it: Jesus, their *Master*, the *Son* of *God*, was doing the work of a *servant*.

When it was Peter's turn, he said, "Oh, no! *You* must not wash my feet!"

But Jesus *did* wash Peter's feet. He washed the feet of *all* His disciples, and dried them with the towel.

When He had finished, He sat down and said, "You call me Master and Lord. I *am* your Master and Lord, yet I have washed your feet. I have washed your feet to show you how *you* must love one another."

If their *Master* loved them so much that He would be their *servant*, then *they* ought to love *one another*. And *we* ought to love one another. We should even be servants for one another!

We must *grow* in love for other people.

SOMETHING TO TALK ABOUT:

In what many ways did Jesus show His love for us?

How can we show love for one another?

If we love others, will we say, "Me first!"?

JESUS SAID:

Love one another, as I have loved you.

JOHN 15:12

SUGGESTED READING:

I John 4:7–11

HYMN

If we love one another, we will do all we can to make others happy. In this hymn we ask God to make us *willing* to be *servants* instead of thinking of ourselves first:

Wake us, O Lord, to human need
To go wherever You would lead.
Awake our senses so that we
More sensitive to needs may be.

Since You've redeemed us from despair,
You've freed us so that we can share;
Our neighbors' problems now we'll bear.
Because You love, we love and care!

TALLIS' CANON
(CH 63; HY 179; JS 109)

(Shall we ask God to help us love one another?)

Dear Jesus, You have loved us so very, very much. Help us to love each other. Help us to put selfishness out of our hearts, because selfishness is sin. Then we will try to make others happy for Jesus' sake. *Amen.*

God's Children Trust Him

God takes care of *everything*. The whole big world is in His hands. The moon and the stars are in His hands. He takes care of the birds and the flowers. He takes care of little children. He takes care of you and of me. He takes care of all His people, and has promised to take care of us *always*.

The Bible tells a story about Peter, how he did something wonderful one day when he *trusted* Jesus, and what happened when he *stopped* trusting Jesus.

Jesus' disciples were in a boat, on the lake. It was night. They had only the moonlight to show them the way to shore. And then a big storm came. The wind began to blow hard. It made the boat go the wrong way, and big waves began to splash into the boat. The disciples were afraid. And Jesus was not with them this time.

While they were trying hard to row the boat, suddenly they saw something on the water, something white and scary. It was moving. It was coming *toward* them. In the dark, they could

not tell what it was. They became terribly frightened. That white thing was even worse than the *storm*!

And then they heard a voice—Jesus' voice! "Do not be afraid!" Jesus said. "It is I!"

Oh, how glad the disciples were! They did not have to be afraid at all. It was *Jesus* coming toward them, walking on the water. He had been near them all the time during the storm, and taking care of them.

Peter said, "If it *really* is You, Jesus, let me walk on the water to meet You."

Jesus said, "Come!"

Peter quickly climbed over the edge of the boat. He kept his eyes on Jesus while he put his feet down on the water. And he *walked* on the water, just as Jesus did, without sinking down.

But suddenly the wind blew harder. A big wave came rolling toward Peter. Peter took his eyes *off* Jesus, and looked at the *wave*. And then he was *afraid*. And he began to sink down, down. . . .

"O Lord, *help* me!" he cried.

Jesus caught Peter's hand. He held Peter up. He said, "Why did you not trust Me?" Then they went back to the boat together.

Wasn't it wonderful, how Peter could walk on the water while he trusted Jesus? He began to sink *only* when he took his eyes off Jesus and *stopped* trusting Him.

We should *always* trust Jesus.

Peter should not have been afraid at all. He was doing what Jesus had told him to do. When we do what God and Jesus *want* us to do, we need *never* be afraid, no matter what happens. God has *promised* to take care of us, and He always keeps His promises!

Our trust in Jesus must grow stronger and stronger.

SOMETHING TO TALK ABOUT:

How could Peter walk right on top of the water?
What made him begin to sink?
How should we trust God when we are sick?
When we are in the dark?
When we work?
When we play?

THE BIBLE SAYS:

Whoso putteth his trust in the Lord shall be safe.

PROVERBS 29:25

SUGGESTED READING:
Matthew 14:24–31

HERE IS A HYMN ABOUT TRUSTING JESUS:
God of our life,
   through all the circling years,
We trust in Thee;
In all the past,
   through all our hopes and fears,
Thy hand we see.
With each new day,
   when morning lifts the veil,
We own Thy mercies, Lord,
   which never fail.

YATTENDON
(HY 172)

A PRAYER:

Father in heaven, sometimes we are afraid. When we are afraid, help us to remember that Thou art taking care of us. Help us to trust thee, always. *Amen.*

56

God's Children Give

Are you glad when your birthday comes? Your birthday is a *happy* day. Maybe you get *presents*. Maybe Mother gives you a present. Maybe Grandma brings a surprise.

It's fun to get presents, isn't it?

Getting presents makes you happy. But do you know what will make you even *more* happy. *Much* more happy? *Giving* something makes us more happy than *getting* something. We give presents to Mother and Father, and to our brothers and sisters, and to our friends, because we love them. Try it, and see how happy you yourself will be.

Best of all, we can give to *God*. That makes us *especially* happy. Do you remember how Mary gave Jesus that wonderful perfume?

One day, long ago, when the Israelites were God's special people, God told them to build Him a tabernacle—a big tent where they could worship Him. He told Moses, their leader, just how to make it. And He said, "Everybody who *wants* to may bring things for the tabernacle. You may bring gold and silver; you may bring wood and beautiful cloth and animal skins; you may bring jewelry, and sweet incense. . . ."

Do you think many people *wanted* to bring gifts to God, for the tabernacle? Oh, yes! All who *loved* the Lord were *glad* to bring their gifts. They brought many, many things. They brought their *best* things. They brought *so* much that at last Moses said they should stop! Moses had more than enough for the tabernacle. The people had *shown* God how much they loved Him.

Why were they so glad to bring gifts to God?

It was because *He* had done so much for *them*.

God is the great *Giver*. Everything we have *He* has given to us. When *we* give, we are a little bit *like* Him. And that makes us happy.

What can we give? And to *whom* can we give?

First of all, we should give our whole self to God. If we are God's children, we say to God, "I *belong* to You, dear Father." That is most wonderful. That is the gift God loves best.

And then, because we love God, we want to give to *others*. We want to *share* all the good things we have. We give to the poor, because Jesus loves them. We give to help missionaries tell the story of Jesus everywhere. We give kind words and do kind deeds to people around us, as Jesus did.

Jesus says that when we give something to someone else because we love Jesus, we are really giving to Jesus *Himself*. Isn't it wonderful, that we can really give something to Jesus, just as Mary gave her precious perfume? We, too, can show Jesus how much we love Him.

And all this giving will make us *happy*.

Our giving must grow and grow.

SOMETHING TO TALK ABOUT:
What should we give to God first of all?
How can we give something to Jesus?
Why does giving make us happy?

OUR LORD JESUS ALSO SAID:
It is more blessed to give than to receive.
ACTS 20:35

We should give, and give, and give. If we give because we love Jesus, we will be very happy. And God will give us more than we can ever even ask for! He will give us joy forever!

SUGGESTED READING:
Matthew 10:42

How can we do that?

HYMN:

Because I have been given much,
  I too must give;
Because of Thy great bounty, Lord,
  each day I live,
I shall divide my gifts from Thee
With every brother that I see
Who has the need of help from me.

Because I have been sheltered, fed,
  by Thy good care,
I cannot see another's lack and I not share
My glowing fire, my loaf of bread,
My roof's safe shelter overhead,
That he, too, may be comforted.

BARBARA
(HY 31)

A PRAYER:

Father in heaven, we give Thee praise because Thou art great and holy and glorious. We give our hearts to Thee, too. We give all that we have to Thee, because we belong to Thee and we love Thee. We are so glad that we can give something to our dear Father and to our dear Saviour. *Amen.*

God's Children Obey

The Bible tells us about a king named Saul. He was king of God's people, the Israelites. He was a big tall man. He was brave, too. He was a good soldier. The people were happy when God made him king.

One day Samuel, God's prophet, said to Saul,

"God wants you to go and fight against the Amalek people. They have been wicked and cruel. When you win the battle, you must not keep *any* of their sheep or camels or other animals. You must kill them all."

Saul called his soldiers together, and they

went away to war. God used Saul to punish the wicked people of Amalek. Saul and his soldiers won the battle, and they were very happy.

But at night God spoke to Samuel. He said, "Saul did not obey Me."

Samuel was sorry. He wondered what Saul had *done*. In the morning he went away to the camp of the army.

When Samuel came near to the camp, he heard a noise. He stood still to listen. It was the bleating of sheep he heard—Baaa! Baaa! And the mooing of cattle—Mooo! Mooo! *Then* he knew what Saul had done!

Samuel hurried on. Soon he found Saul. Saul was glad to see Samuel. He said, "I have done just what the Lord told me to do."

But Samuel said, "What about the noise I hear—the bleating of sheep and the mooing of cattle?"

"Oh," Saul said, "my men kept the best animals. They want to give them to the Lord. They will give them to the Lord as sacrifices."

Samuel shook his head. "God told you not to keep *any* of the animals," he said. "You did not *obey* God. And because you did not obey Him, He will take the kingdom away from you."

Then Saul was sorry. He learned too late that it is *very important* to obey God. To *obey* is even more important than to *give* to God. Think of it!

We may give much money to God. We may give Him big presents. But if we *really love* Him we will *obey* Him. That is the most important way to show Him that we love Him.

God gave a very special commandment that children must remember. He said to children, *"Obey your parents in the Lord."* That means, obey your parents because the *Lord* wants you to obey them. When you obey *them*, you obey *Him*. Jesus obeyed *His* parents on earth, and He obeyed His Father in heaven, too.

We must grow in obedience.

SOMETHING TO TALK ABOUT:
Why did Saul disobey God?

How did Samuel know that Saul was disobedient?

Can we really love God and disobey Him?

Why must children obey their parents?

MEMORY VERSE
Everybody should remember what Samuel said to Saul:

> *To obey is better than sacrifice.*
> I SAMUEL 15:22

SUGGESTED READING:
John 15:8–12

HYMN
The hymn that tells us to *trust* God also tells us to *obey* Him. If we do not obey Him, we cannot be happy in Him:

> When we walk with the Lord
>   in the light of His Word,
> What a glory He sheds on our way!
> While we do His good will
>   He abides with us still,
> And with all who will trust and obey.
> Trust and obey, for there's no other way
> To be happy in Jesus but to trust and obey.
>
> Then in fellowship sweet
>   we will sit at His feet,
> Or we'll walk by His side in the way;
> What He says we will do,
>   where He sends we will go.
> Never fear, only trust and obey.
> Trust and obey, for there's no other way
> To be happy in Jesus but to trust and obey.
> TRUST AND OBEY
> (JS 137)

A PRAYER:
Dear Lord Jesus, we know that we ought to be obedient. If we trust and obey You, we will be happy. Help us to know what You want us to do, and help us to obey. *Amen.*

God's Children Work

Did you ever see little kittens play? Kittens like to run and jump. They like to chase a ball. They like to roll on the floor.

Other little animals play too—puppies, baby bears, little lambs—they all play.

And *children* like to play.

But children have *work* to do. Children should not play *all* the time. As soon as boys and girls are big enough, they should help Mother and Daddy with the work. When they grow bigger, there is *more* work for them to do. Grown-ups must work almost *all* the time. They must work because God *says* so.

When God made Adam and Eve, He put them in a beautiful garden. It was like a park. There were flowers and birds; there were trees with all kinds of fruit; there were rivers with clear running water. But Adam and Eve had *work* to do. God said to them, "You must take care of the garden."

Adam and Eve were happy in the garden. They *liked* to work. It was a joy to take care of the trees and bushes, and to keep the whole big garden looking beautiful.

But then sin came. You know how Adam and Eve listened to Satan. They disobeyed God. After *that*, work was *hard*. God sent Adam and Eve out of the garden. They had to dig in the ground. They had to plant seeds. They had to pull weeds. Weeds grow very fast! And there were thorny weeds that pricked.

We have to work hard too, sometimes. And sometimes the work makes us tired. But work is *good* for us.

Work makes us *strong*. When we work, our bodies grow strong.

Work makes us *happy*. We *like* to make things. It's a *joy* to get our work done *well*.

We can work to help other people, and make *them* happy.

Best of all, we can work for *God*. If we do our work well, He will be pleased. And if we think of *Him* while we do our work, we will be happy even though our work may be hard. It's wonderful to work for Him.

Taking care of God's creation—birds and trees and flowers and animals—is still part of the work we must do.

SOMETHING TO TALK ABOUT:
What work can you do for Mother and Daddy?
How can you work for God?
What work did Jesus do?
Why is work good for us?

ONE OF GOD'S COMMANDMENTS SAYS:
Six days shalt thou labour, and do all thy work.
EXODUS 20:9

SUGGESTED READING:
II Thessalonians 3:10–12

HERE IS A HYMN ABOUT WORK:
Come, labor on.
Who dares stand idle on the harvest plain,
While all around him waves the golden
  grain?
And to each servant does the master say,
"Go work today."
ORA LABORA
(HY 149)

A PRAYER:
Dear Father in heaven, forgive us when we do not like to work. Jesus had work to do, and we have work to do. Help us to do our work for Thee, every day. *Amen.*

God's Children Read the Bible

When boys and girls go to school, they learn to *read*. They learn to read *books*.

There are many good books to read. There are thousands and thousands of them. And we *want* to read good books, because there is so *much* to *learn*.

There is *one* book that *everybody* should read. That book is the *Bible*. The Bible is the *most* important of all the thousands and thousands of books. Why is the Bible such an important book? Well, it is *God's* book. It is the *only* book that

God has written for us. It is the *only* book that tells us who we are, and what we are here on earth for. Without the *Bible*, we would not really understand anything at all!

God began to have the Bible written long ago, in the time of Moses. You remember some of the stories about Moses. When he was a baby, His mother put him in a basket in the river, and the princess of Egypt found him. Moses became the great leader of God's people.

This Moses was a man who loved God very

119

much. *Two* times he spent forty days alone with God, on a mountain.

God used *Moses* to begin His book for us. God the Holy Spirit guided Moses, telling him just what to write. Moses wrote all about how God made heaven and earth, and how God made everything that is on the earth. He wrote about Adam and Eve, how wonderfully they were made, and how they disobeyed God. Moses wrote about God's people, the Israelites, how God made them *His* people, and took care of them.

Afterwards God chose other men to write more. They told about a Saviour who was going to come. We call these men prophets.

And then God chose still other men, some of them Jesus' own disciples, to write how the Saviour came and what He did for us.

The Bible is a *big* book. We cannot read it all in one day. We should read a little *every* day. Then we will learn all that God wants us to know about Him. The Bible is such a wonderful book, that we can read a little every day until we are *very* old and we will always be learning *still more* about God. We will learn what a great God He is, and how we can live for Him.

It is good to memorize parts of the Bible. Then we *grow* in every good way.

SOMETHING TO TALK ABOUT:

Why should all boys and girls learn to read?

Why is the Bible the most important book to read?

How can we help people in other lands read the Bible?

MEMORY VERSE

God's children *love* the Bible. They *want* to read it. The prophet Jeremiah said:

Thy word was unto me the joy and rejoicing of mine heart.

JEREMIAH 15:16

SUGGESTED READING:

Deuteronomy 11:18–21

HYMN:

Thy Word sheds light upon my path;
A shining light, it guides my feet;
Thy righteous judgments to observe
My solemn vow I now repeat.

ROCKINGHAM
(HY 49)

A PRAYER:

Father in heaven, we thank Thee for that most wonderful book, the Bible. Send Thy Spirit into our hearts, to help us understand it and love it more and more. May we never, never forget to read it, for we cannot know Thee unless we read it over and over, and the more we read it the better we will know Thee. *Amen.*

120

God's Children
Think About God

Have you heard about David, the shepherd boy? The Bible tells us about him. He took care of his father's sheep.

David took the sheep far from home, to find good green grass for them. Sometimes he took them to a green valley between high hills. He watched them *all* day long. When they were thirsty, he led them to still waters to get a drink. He always watched to see that there was no *bear* or *lion* near by, to catch a sheep or a lamb.

Sometimes, when the sheep rested, David had time to sit down. Then he took his harp and began to play. David made sweet music with his harp, and he made up many songs to sing. David made up many songs about God.

You see, David was always *thinking* about God. He looked at the hills all around him, and he thought about God who had placed them there. When he saw the flowers in the grass, and when he heard the birds sing, he thought about God who made them so beautiful and so wonderful. At night, when the sheep were in the fold, David looked up at the stars. Then he thought how *great* God is, and how high and holy.

David thought about God very, very often. And so he grew up to be a great man of God. And God *loved* David very much.

We should think about God *every* day, and many times a day. If we think of Him while we work and while we play, we will try to *please* Him. We *should* try to please God, our Father, and Jesus, our dear Saviour, in *all* that we do. Then we, too, will grow up to be strong sons and daughters of God.

If we think of God while we play, we will not be selfish, or cross, or angry. We will be kind and loving and good. If we think of God while we work, we will do our work well. Remember, He is our Father, our *heavenly* Father, and He loves us very much! And Jesus, our dear Saviour, loves us very, very much, too.

If we think of Him often, how *can* we be naughty? And how can we be disobedient? Or afraid, even in the dark at night?

Christians should think of God very, very often. They should sing His praises, when they remember how He loves them. Then they will be happy Christians.

Paul, the great missionary, said, "For me to live is Christ." The love of Jesus *filled* his heart and mind, so that his whole life was lived for Jesus. That is why he could be happy even in time of trouble. His mind was full of thoughts of Jesus.

Thinking about God makes our new heart grow strong in love and holiness.

SOMETHING TO TALK ABOUT:

What did you see today that made you think of God?

How did Paul live for Christ?

Why does thinking on God make us happy?

THE PROPHET ISAIAH SAID:

Thou wilt keep him in perfect peace, whose mind is stayed on thee.

ISAIAH 26:3

SUGGESTED READING:
Psalm 77:11–14

What does "meditate" mean?

HYMN:

O Master, let me walk with Thee
In lowly paths of service free;
Tell me Thy secret, help me bear
The strain of toil, the fret of care.

In hope that sends a shining ray
Far down the future's broadening way,
In peace that only Thou canst give,
With Thee, O Master, let me live.

MARYTON
(HY 142)

A PRAYER:

Dear Father, we know that if we take time to think about You, we will become more like You. Help us to understand how wonderful it is to fill our minds with thoughts about You and Your Son Jesus. *Amen*.

God's Children Learn to Say "No"

Sometimes God's children are tempted to do wrong. Do you know what you must say if someone tells you to do something wrong? You must say "No!"

Sometimes it is very hard to say "No."

One day, long ago, a wicked king made a great big idol. He told all his people that they must kneel to the idol. He said it was a *god*.

All the people gathered around. It was a great crowd. Then the king's servant shouted: "When

122

the *band* begins to play, you must all bow down!"

Soon the band began to play. Did *all* those people fall down on their knees, as if that idol was a god? Oh, no!—not *all* the people. *Three* young men did *not* bow their knees. They stood straight and tall.

Of course, when the king saw them, he was angry. He said, "Who are those young men who dare to stay standing when I told them to kneel? Bring them to me!"

His servants brought the three young men— Shadrach, Meshach, and Abednego.

The king said to them, "I have a furnace with a very hot fire. If you do not kneel to my idol, I will have you thrown into that furnace! Now, the band will play again, and *you must kneel down!*"

The young men shook their heads. They said, "No, O King. We serve the *living God*. We cannot bow down to an idol and sin against our God. When the band plays, we will *not* bow down, and our God will take care of us."

They were *brave* young men. They dared to say "No" to the king! It was not easy! They knew he would throw them into that hot fire.

And he *did*. He was so angry! But oh, how wonderful! God sent an angel to take care of them. The fire did not harm them at all!

The Bible tells us about these three young men because they dared to say "No." And the Bible tells us that the great king, Nebuchadnezzar, *praised God* when he saw how God took care of the brave young men.

Sometimes *we* have to say "No."

Sometimes we want to do something Mother has told us not to do. Then we must say, "No, I will not disobey Mother."

Sometimes *playmates* tempt us to do something that is not right. Then we must say "No" to them.

Sometimes *Satan* tries to makes us disobey Mother or Daddy. Then we must say "No" to *him*.

Every time we are tempted to do wrong, we must say "No." Then we will become *strong* children of God.

SOMETHING TO TALK ABOUT:
What does "temptation" mean?
Who tempts us to do wrong?
What must we do when it's hard to say "No"?

PAUL ONCE WROTE TO HIS FRIENDS:
Be strong in the Lord.

EPHESIANS 6:10

Sometimes it is hard to say "No," but the Lord Jesus will help us when we ask Him.

SUGGESTED READING:
Daniel 3:19–29

HYMN

When we are tempted to do *wrong*, we can ask Jesus to help us. Here is a song to sing to Him:

Father, lead me day by day
Ever in Thine own sweet way;
Teach me to be pure and true,
Show me what I ought to do.

When I'm tempted to do wrong,
Make me steadfast, wise, and strong;
And when all alone I stand,
Shield me with Thy mighty hand.

BUCKLAND
(CH 156)

PRAYER:
Lord Jesus, sometimes I am tempted to do wrong. Help me to say "No." Make me strong to do the right, so that I will please Thee. Help other boys and girls, too, so that we will be happy together in Thee. *Amen*.

123

God's Children
Tell God's Story

Simon and his brother Andrew went fishing. They had a boat in the Sea of Galilee. And they had a big net. They always fished with nets.

When they had rowed a little way from shore, they let the net down into the water. Simon held one end. Andrew held the other end.

Suddenly, while they were busy with the net, they heard somebody call: "Simon! Andrew!"

They looked around, and they saw a man standing on shore. It was *Jesus*. He was calling them.

"Come and follow Me!" Jesus said, "and I will make you fishers of men!"

Fishers of men? Simon and Andrew did not know what Jesus meant. But they pulled up their net and they rowed to shore. They got out of their boat, and they went with Jesus.

Not far away some other men were in another boat. James and his brother John were there, mending their nets. Their father, Zebedee, was with them. Jesus stopped by their boat and said, "Come, follow Me!"

Then James and John left their nets, and *they* followed Jesus.

Jesus wanted Simon and Andrew and James and John to be *fishers of men*. Do you know what that means?

Ever since they were little boys, they had been catching fish in their nets. They brought some fish home to eat. The rest they sold. They knew just how to handle the nets to catch fish.

Now Jesus told them that they must catch *men*, and bring them into the Kingdom of Heaven. That was a *different* kind of fishing. Jesus was going to send them into the big wide world to get *people*, and bring people to Him.

Jesus *did* make them fishers of men. First they went to school with Jesus, to learn *how* to catch men. And then they became preachers and missionaries. They told the story of salvation, to bring all kinds of people into the Kingdom of Heaven.

Just before He went to heaven, Jesus said to *all* His disciples, "Go ye into all the world and preach the gospel." So He made them all fishers of men.

If we belong to Jesus, and the Holy Spirit lives in our hearts, *we* must be fishers of men, too. We must tell others about Jesus, so that others will come to the Kingdom of Heaven. There are still so many who do *not know* Jesus and who have *never* heard of His wonderful love. They do not know that He died for our sins and will make us children of God. We want to do all we can to tell them God's wonderful story. When we do that, we are fishers of men.

We *grow* when we learn how to be fishers of men.

SOMETHING TO TALK ABOUT:

How can we be "fishers of men"?
What should we tell people about Jesus?

MEMORY VERSE

Let's remember what Jesus said to His disciples
just before He went to heaven:

Go ye therefore, and teach all nations.

MATTHEW 28:19

SUGGESTED READING:

Matthew 28:16–20

HYMN:

> There are many children
> Who have never heard
> Of His love and tender care,
> Of His holy Word.
>
> I will help these children
> Learn of Jesus' love
> So that He may welcome them
> To His home above.

ALLE JAHRE WIEDER
(CH 147; JS 12)

PRAYER:

Lord Jesus, speak to us, and call us to be
fishers of men. Tell us just what we should tell
others about Thee. Bless the missionaries who
go to faraway lands to tell the story, so that people everywhere may know about Thee. *Amen.*

God's Children
Suffer for Him

God's children are very happy when they know that Jesus loves them. But sometimes they have to *suffer* for Jesus' sake. Very many of God's people have suffered for Jesus' sake.

After Jesus was gone to heaven, His disciples began telling people how Jesus died for our sins. Many people believed in Jesus. They became Christians.

Stephen was a fine young man. He heard the disciples tell the story of Jesus, and he *believed*. He loved Jesus. The Holy Spirit filled Stephen's heart so that he loved Jesus *very* much. Then Stephen began to tell *others* about Jesus. He wanted everybody to know the wonderful story. He became a "fisher of men"!

The wicked men who had killed Jesus heard Stephen preach about Jesus. They did not want more people to believe. So they hired some men to tell lies about Stephen.

These men said, "Stephen is a bad man. He says terrible things about God, things that are all wrong."

Stephen was not afraid. He went right on telling people that Jesus was the only Saviour, and that they must believe in Him.

But the wicked men took hold of Stephen and dragged him out of the city. They threw him down in the road. Then they began to throw stones at him. They kept on throwing big stones until they had *killed* Stephen.

Stephen's friends could not help him. They could only watch. They saw Stephen kneel down, just before he died. They saw him look up to the sky, and they saw his face shine like the face of an *angel*! They heard him say, "I see Jesus!" And they heard him say, "Lord Jesus, receive my spirit!" Then Stephen died. His friends cried when they buried Stephen. They were very sad that Stephen had had to suffer so. But they knew Stephen *could* not stop telling about Jesus, no matter *how* much the stones hurt. And they knew his heart was full of joy when he saw Jesus. They knew, too, that while they buried his *body*, his *soul* was with Jesus.

What made the wicked men hate Stephen so? *Satan* filled their hearts with hatred. Satan is God's enemy, you know. He does not *want* us to tell about God's love and the love of Jesus.

Jesus had *told* His disciples that they would have to suffer for Him. He also had told them that this would make them *happy*.

A Christian must truly love God to suffer so for Him.

SOMETHING TO TALK ABOUT:
Did Stephen deserve to be stoned? Had He done wrong?

Must we stop talking about Jesus when people tell us to?

What did Stephen see that made him happy?

JESUS SAID:

Blessed are ye, when men shall . . . persecute you.

MATTHEW 5:11

SUGGESTED READING:
Acts 7:54–60

All God's children must suffer for Jesus at least a little bit. People who do not love Him will not like us. Some may poke fun of us and laugh at us. Some of God's children have suffered *very much* for His sake. Many have *died*, just as Stephen did. Those who loved God very much were *happy* when they suffered for Jesus' sake, just as Stephen was.

HYMN:

Our fathers, chained in prisons dark,
Were still in heart and conscience free;
How sure will be their children's peace
If they, like them, contend for Thee!
Faith of our fathers, holy faith!
We will be true to Thee till death.

ST. CATHERINE
(HY 136)

A PRAYER:

Lord Jesus, we do not know for sure if we could be happy if we had to suffer for Thee. We are afraid. But help us, dear Lord. We do not like to suffer, but if we must suffer for Thee as Stephen did, then make us happy in Thee, and make us brave. *Amen.*

God's Children Look for What Is Coming

When Paul, the great missionary, was an old man, he was put in jail in Rome. He was there a long time. The wicked ruler of Rome set soldiers to watch him. And after a while he *killed* Paul.

What had Paul done that was wrong?

Oh, he was not put in jail because he did something *wrong*. He was put in jail because he preached about *Jesus*, just like Stephen. People who hated God wanted to make Paul *stop* telling the story of Jesus. And so they told lies about him and had him put in jail.

What do you think Paul *did* in jail?

He kept *right on* talking about Jesus. He even told the soldiers who watched him about Jesus. Friends came to see him, and he talked to them about Jesus. And he wrote letters—big long letters—to the churches, telling them how to live for Jesus and how to be happy in Him.

Paul did not grumble about his troubles. Do you know what he said? He said: "My troubles do not matter at all! They will last just a little while, and I am looking for wonderful things that God will give me when all my troubles are gone!" He said: "If I must *die*, I will go to Jesus, and that is the very best that can happen to me! Jesus arose from the dead, and He will raise *me* from the dead. He will give me a *new* body. And I shall live with Him in *glory, forever*!"

It is wonderful to be a child of God. A child of God can be happy *anywhere*. If we have troubles, we know they will last only a little while. We know they are good for us. We think of what is coming. We think of the place in heaven that Jesus is making ready for us.

Paul *knew* that he was going to die. But he was not afraid. He was sure that Jesus would *never* stop loving him. He was sure that Jesus would take him to heaven. He looked ahead, to the wonderful things that would come, and he was happy.

We, too, should look for what is *coming*. Then the troubles of today will not make us unhappy. It does not matter if we are poor. We are going to be *rich* some day! We are rich *already*, if we have *Jesus*. It does not matter if we are sick. We are going to be all better, and *never* be sick again, in heaven. It does not matter if people laugh at us. We are going to be happy forever, with Jesus, when He takes us to be with Him.

God has done wonderful things for us already. He has given us a way of salvation in Jesus. And there are still more wonderful things to come—things *so* wonderful that we cannot even imagine what they are.

When we think of all this, we want to be good; we want to grow more and more like Jesus.

SOMETHING TO TALK ABOUT:
Can anything stop Jesus' love for us?
How do we know He will always love us?
What is He making ready for us?

128

THE BIBLE SAYS:

Eye hath not seen, nor ear heard . . . the things which God hath prepared for them that love him.

I CORINTHIANS 2:9

SUGGESTED READING:
I John 3:1–3

We grow more and more like Jesus as long as we live on earth. But when we see Him we shall really be like Him.

A HYMN TO SING:

> And our eyes at last shall see Him
> Through His own redeeming love,
> For the child so dear and gentle
> Is our Lord in heaven above;
> And He leads His children on
> To the place where He is gone.
>
> Not in that poor lowly stable
> With the oxen standing by,
> We shall see Him; but in heaven,
> Set at God's right hand on high;
> Where like stars His children crowned
> All in white shall wait around.

IRBY
(CH 92)

A PRAYER:

Lord Jesus, we are so glad that nothing can stop Your love for us. We want to grow more and more like You. And we are so happy when we think of the wonderful things You are making ready for us in heaven! *Amen.*

MEMORY VERSES OF PART TEN

If any man be in Christ, he is a new creature.
II CORINTHIANS 5:17

We love him, because he first loved us.
I JOHN 4:19

Love one another, as I have loved you.
JOHN 15:12

Whoso putteth his trust in the Lord shall be safe.
PROVERBS 29:25

It is more blessed to give than to receive.

ACTS 20:35

To obey is better than sacrifice.

I SAMUEL 15:22

Six days shalt thou labour, and do all thy work.

EXODUS 20:9

Thy word was unto me the joy and rejoicing of mine heart.

JEREMIAH 15:16

Thou wilt keep him in perfect peace, whose mind is stayed on thee.

ISAIAH 26:3

Be strong in the Lord.

EPHESIANS 6:10

Go ye therefore, and teach all nations.

MATTHEW 28:19

Blessed are ye, when men shall . . . persecute you.

MATTHEW 5:11

Eye hath not seen, nor ear heard . . . the things which God hath
prepared for them that love him.

I CORINTHIANS 2:9

PART ELEVEN
·
God Helps
His Children
Live For Him

We Need Help, to Live for God

Sometimes Mother says to you, "Now I expect you to be a *good* girl, or a *good* boy."

Then you tell her you *will* be good. And you do *want* to be good. But oh, very often you are naughty after all!

And sometimes you even *want* to be naughty!

If we are God's children, *He* expects us to be good.

God says to us, "You must love Me best of all." And He also says, "You must love others just as much as you love yourself."

But *very often* we forget to love God best of all. And how selfish we are! We love *ourselves* best, instead of loving others just as much as we love ourselves.

God says you must not tell lies, you must not be angry, you must not be cross, or selfish, or disobedient. But we *are*. Oh, very often!

Even *Paul*, the great missionary, was not good all the time.

And King David, who loved God so much, was not always good.

Nobody is good all the time.

Why is it so hard to be good?

It is hard because *sin* is *strong*, even when we have a new heart. Our hearts are full of seeds of sin and they grow so fast! They are like weed seeds.

Do you sometimes help Mother weed the garden? You can pull out all the weeds today, but tomorrow new weeds are growing again. Where do they *come* from? They come from *seeds* that are in the ground.

The *seeds* of *sin* are in our hearts. And they keep coming up. Jesus forgives our sins when we ask Him every day, but the next day we sin again. Even if we have *new* hearts, the seeds of sin still try to grow. So we *cannot* be good all the time.

It is very sad. We should *always* live for God and praise Him, but we *cannot*. Sometimes we do not even *want* to. That is the worst of all the weed seeds.

Paul, the great missionary, when he wrote a letter to his friends in Rome, told them he was very unhappy when he thought about the sin that kept coming up in his heart. He said, "I do not *want* to sin, but I *do* sin."

Peter, who was so brave, and would not stop telling about Jesus even though he was put in jail, knew that sin still grew in his heart.

SOMETHING TO TALK ABOUT:

What are some of the weeds of sin that grew in your heart today?

MEMORY VERSE:

John, the disciple who loved Jesus very much, wrote this:

If we say that we have no sin, we deceive ourselves, and the truth is not in us.

I JOHN 1:8

If sin is so strong, and the weeds of sin keep coming up in our hearts, what can we do? We need *help*. We want to get *rid* of sin!

In our next lessons we will learn how God helps us.

SUGGESTED READING:
I John 1:7–2:1

HYMN:

> Did we in our own strength confide,
> Our striving would be losing;
> Were not the right man on our side,
> The man of God's own choosing.
> Dost ask who that may be?
> Christ Jesus, it is He;
> Lord Sabaoth His name,
> From age to age the same,
> And He must win the battle.

And though this world, with devils filled,
Should threaten to undo us,
We will not fear, for God hath willed
His truth to triumph through us.
The prince of darkness grim,
We tremble not for him;
His rage we can endure,
For lo! his doom is sure;
One little word shall fell him.

EIN FESTE BURG
(HY 37; JS 150)

PRAYER
(Now shall we fold our hands and ask God to forgive and help us?)

Father in heaven, we want to be good, and we try to be good. But often we are naughty. Forgive our sins today for Jesus' sake. And help us to pull the weeds of sin out of our hearts. We need Thy help, because we cannot do it alone. *Amen.*

66

The Father Will Help If We Ask Him

Jesus told His disciples that the Father will give us every good thing we ask for. And He will surely help us to be *good*, if we ask Him.

Jesus told His disciples a little story. He said: "Suppose a friend should come to visit you late at night. He has come from far away, and he is hungry. You want to give him something to eat, but you have no bread in the house. And at night the stores are closed.

"Then you will go to the house of another friend, to ask *him* for bread. You knock at the door. Your friend wakes up. You call to him, 'My friend, can you let me have some bread? I have a visitor, and he is hungry, and I have nothing for him to eat.'

"What will your friend say? Will he say, 'Oh, don't bother me. We are all in bed. I don't want to get up and give you bread'?

"No, he will not say that. If he is really your *friend* he will get up and he will give you all the bread you need."

Jesus told the disciples that *God* is like that. God will *never* say, "Don't bother Me." He will not say "No" when we ask for something we need. God is our *very best* Friend. God is even *more* than that; He is our *Father* in heaven, and He loves us. He will surely give us the good things we ask for.

Our Father in heaven *knows* that it is hard for us to be good all the time. He *knows* it is hard for us to live for Him the way we should. He knows that we are weak and sinful. But He *wants* us to live for Him. And He is glad to *help* us pull the weeds of sin out of our hearts.

First we must *tell* Him about those weeds of sin, and just *what* they are. Then we must ask Him to *help* us. We must ask Him to make us *want* to pull them out. We must ask Him to make us *strong* to do what is right.

We must ask Him to make us strong to say *"No"* to all that is wrong.

We must ask Him to fill our hearts with *love*. If we love Him very, very much, it is *not* so hard to be good.

We must ask Him for the *Holy Spirit*, to live in our hearts and to *lead* us in the right way; to make us *strong* to live for our Father in heaven, and for Jesus.

God will *give* us all these things if we ask Him, because He has promised to give us *whatever* is good for us. But we must really, *really* want to be good.

SOMETHING TO TALK ABOUT:

Does God give us everything we ask for?
What will He surely give us?
How does He know what is good for us?

JESUS SAID:

Ask, and it shall be given you; seek, and ye shall find.

MATTHEW 7:7

SUGGESTED READING:
I John 5:12–15

HYMN:

Let us with a gladsome mind
Praise the Lord, for He is kind;
For His mercies aye endure,
Ever faithful, ever sure.

All things living He doth feed;
His full hand supplies their need;
For His mercies aye endure,
Ever faithful, ever sure.

LOUEZ DIEU TOUT HAUTEMENT
(HY 10)

PRAYER:

Dear Father in heaven, Thou knowest that we want to live for Thee. Make us strong to do what is right. Make us strong to say "No" to all that is wrong. Fill our hearts with love for Thee, and send the Holy Spirit to lead us in the right ways, for Jesus' sake. *Amen*.

The Holy Spirit Helps Us

Jesus said He would "abide" in us. He also sent the Holy Spirit to live in us.

It is especially God the Holy Spirit who helps us to be good. The Holy Spirit tells us what to do.

Paul, the missionary, went to many cities to tell the story of Jesus. He went to Galatia, too. And many people in Galatia believed the gospel. They became Christians. Then, of course, they wanted to live for God.

But after a while, when Paul was gone, the people of Galatia began to quarrel. They *forgot* to live as God's children ought to live. They did not love one another as they should. Some were selfish, and some were jealous.

Paul heard about this. He was sorry that they did not do good. He wrote them a letter. We can read that letter. It is in the Bible—Paul's *Letter to the Galatians*.

In that letter Paul told the Galatians that they should not quarrel, and that they must stop being selfish and jealous. Then he told them how God would help them.

Paul wrote to them: If you *walk* in the *Spirit*, you will not do such things. If you walk in the Spirit you will show the *fruits* of the Spirit.

What did Paul mean?

Well, you know that a good apple tree will bear good apples. And a good pear tree will bear good pears. *Our* good fruits are the good things that come out of our hearts—love, kindness, truth, happiness, and all other good things. And we *can* have those good fruits if the *Holy Spirit* lives in our hearts. He lives in the heart of everyone who loves Jesus, you know.

But sometimes we do *not* have such fruits. Sometimes God's children bear bad fruits—anger, jealousy, hatred—like a bad tree, and like

SOMETHING TO TALK ABOUT:
What did you do today that was *not* good?
How can we keep from being naughty tomorrow?
Who is the Holy Spirit?

MEMORY VERSE
Paul also told the Galatians what *kind* of fruits we will bear if we walk in the Spirit. He wrote:

The fruit of the Spirit is love, joy, peace.
GALATIANS 5:22

SUGGESTED READING:
John 15:1–5

Jesus and the Holy Spirit help us bear good fruit.

HYMN
Shall we sing a prayer to the Holy Spirit?

Gracious Spirit, Dove Divine,
Let Thy light within me shine;
All my guilty fears remove,
Fill me with Thy heavenly love.

Life and peace to me impart,
Seal salvation in my heart;
Dwell Thyself within my breast
And bestow eternal rest.

CULBACH
(CH 143; HY 108)

the Galatians did. Now, says Paul, if you would just *listen* to the Holy Spirit, and do what He *tells* you to do, you would bear *good* fruit instead of bad fruit. That is what Paul meant when he told the Galatians to *walk* in the Spirit.

We cannot live for God at *all* without the help of the Holy Spirit. He makes us *want* to be good. He tells us *how* to be good. He tells us through God's Word, the Bible. When we *read* it, He helps us understand what it means and how we must live.

OUR PRAYER:
Holy Spirit, help us to listen to Thee and walk on the right way. Help us to understand the Bible when we read it, so that we will know how to live for our Father in heaven and to please our dear Saviour. *Amen.*

Jesus Prays
for Us

God the Father helps us live for Him, if we ask Him. The Holy Spirit helps us when we walk in the Spirit. And Jesus, God's Son, helps us, too. Jesus *prays* for us. He prays for all His children.

We cannot see Jesus. He is in heaven. But *He* sees *us*. He looks down from heaven. He sees all that we do. He sees right into our hearts. He *lives* in our hearts. He knows when we love Him, and when we *want* to be good.

And He prays for us. He asks God the Father to keep us from sin.

One day, when Jesus was still on earth, He said to Peter: "Satan wants to have you. He is going to try to get you. But I have prayed for you!"

Jesus prayed for Peter because He did not want Satan to get Peter. Jesus *loved* Peter.

Peter *did* sin against Jesus. He *denied* Jesus. He was afraid, and so he said he did not even *know* Jesus. That made Jesus sad.

But after he sinned, Peter was sorry. He was so sorry that he cried. And Jesus forgave Peter. Peter still belonged to Jesus. Satan did *not* get him, even though he led him into sin against Jesus.

After that, Peter loved Jesus more than ever. He was thankful that Jesus had prayed for him. He was thankful that Satan did not get him.

Before Jesus went away to heaven, He talked with His disciples a long time. He told them that He was going to heaven to prepare a place for them. And then He prayed with them. He prayed *for* them, too. And He prayed for *us*.

And even *now* He prays for us. Just think of it—Jesus, up in heaven, sees us down here and prays for us. He knows just what we need. He knows just when we are tempted to do wrong. He knows how hard we try to do right. He sees us when we sin. He asks the Father to keep us from sin, to make us love one another, and to make us holy.

SOMETHING TO TALK ABOUT:
Where is Jesus?
What is He doing?
How does He help us to live for God?

MEMORY VERSE
This is what Jesus said in His prayer to the Father:

I pray for them . . . which thou hast given me; for they are thine . . . and thine are mine.
JOHN 17:9, 10

SUGGESTED READING:
John 17:9–15

Jesus once said He would be our Shepherd. And He *is* our Shepherd, even *now*, although He is in heaven. He watches over us, and He prays for us, as this song says:

Loving Shepherd of Thy sheep,
Keep Thy lamb, in safety keep;
Nothing can Thy power withstand;
None can pluck me from Thy hand.

Loving Shepherd, ever near,
Teach Thy lamb Thy voice to hear;
Suffer not my steps to stray
From the straight and narrow way.

ORIENTIS PARTIBUS
(CH 23; JS 55)

PRAYER:

Jesus, loving Shepherd, keep on praying for us, please, so that we will try hard to be good, and live for Thee. Help us to love Thee best of all, and to love others as much as we love ourselves. *Amen*.

Angels Watch Over Us

You have never seen an angel. And I have never seen an angel.

Angels are *spirits*. We cannot *see* spirits.

Many years ago, when God had a special message, He sometimes sent an angel down to earth to tell that message. Then He gave the angel a *body*, so that people *could* see him.

You remember how an angel came to tell the shepherds that Jesus was born. And then they saw a great *host* of angels, singing in the sky. There are very, very many angels.

138

The angels are God's *helpers*. They are His servants. The Bible tells us that God *still* sends angels sometimes to help His people, even though we never see them.

When God brought His people Israel out of Egypt, many, many years ago, He sent an angel to lead the way. He made a big cloud that all the people could see. The angel was in the cloud. When the angel moved the cloud, the people followed. When the angel made the cloud stand still, the people rested.

One day the king of Egypt and all his soldiers chased after the people of Israel. King Pharaoh wanted to make God's people his slaves again. Then the angel moved the cloud *behind* the Israelites. The cloud stood between the Israelites and the Egyptians, so that the Egyptians could not hurt the Israelites.

Angels do many wonderful things. An angel rolled the stone away from the tomb after Jesus arose from the grave. Then Jesus' friends could see that the grave was empty. Some of the women who came to the grave *saw* the angel, and he told them that Jesus was alive.

Once Peter was put in prison because he preached about Jesus. Peter's friends thought they would never see him again. They prayed for him. That night, while Peter was asleep in prison, he felt someone tap his side. He looked, and there was an angel! The angel loosened the chains that were on Peter's hands. And he opened the prison door for Peter. The guards did not even hear Peter go out. And Peter's friends—how happy they were when Peter came to them!

Jesus once told His disciples that there are *special* angels watching over God's children. Isn't that wonderful? The Father in heaven tells them how to take care of the children.

When we think of all that God does to help us, even sending angels to watch over us, how thankful we are! And how much we want to live

for God, and to please Him! And the more we try to please Him, the *happier* we will be.

Something To Talk About:
Why can't we see angels?
What work do they do for us?
Whom do they obey?

The Bible Says:
He shall give his angels charge over thee, to keep thee in all thy ways.

PSALM 91:11

Suggested Reading:
Acts 12:5–11

Here Is An Evening Hymn:
Now the day is over,
Night is drawing nigh;
Shadows of the evening
Steal across the sky.

Through the long night watches
May Thine angels spread
Their white wings above me,
Watching round my bed.

EUDOXIA
(HY 178)

Dear Father, we thank You for the angels that watch over us. We cannot see them, but we know they are near us, to take care of us, because we belong to You. And we need never be afraid when we know they are watching over us. *Amen.*

MEMORY VERSES OF PART ELEVEN

If we say that we have no sin, we deceive ourselves, and the truth is not in us.
I JOHN 1:8

Ask, and it shall be given you; seek, and ye shall find.
MATTHEW 7:7

The fruit of the Spirit is love, joy, peace.
GALATIANS 5:22

I pray for them . . . which thou hast given me; for they are thine . . . and thine are mine.
JOHN 17:9, 10

He shall give his angels charge over thee, to keep thee in all thy ways.
PSALM 91:11

PART TWELVE
•
When
We Pray
To God

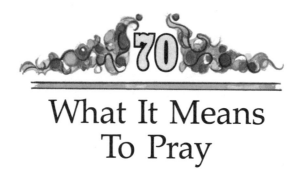

What It Means
To Pray

Do you remember that we learned about God, how *great* He is? And how very *Holy?* And how *almighty, seeing* everything and *knowing* everything?

And yet, although He is so very great and holy, and we are so small and sinful, we may *talk* to Him. When we pray, we talk to Him. And He listens. That is wonderful!

God the Father is Jesus' Father as well as our Father. Jesus is God's very special Son. When Jesus was on earth, He prayed to His Father very often. Sometimes Jesus got up early in the morning, before it was light, to pray. He liked to be alone to talk with His Father. Sometimes he stayed up late at night. Once He went up on a mountain in the evening and talked to God all night long.

God in heaven is *our* Father, too, if we believe in Jesus. And he wants *us* to talk to Him. He wants us to tell Him all about ourselves, what we like, and what we are doing, just as our Daddy and Mother want us to tell *them* everything. We ought to pray to our Father in heaven very often.

He listens to what we say. And then we must listen to what *He* says, just as we listen to Daddy and Mother when we talk with *them*. Our Father in heaven *answers* us. We cannot hear His voice,

but He answers us through His Word, the Bible. And often He answers us in our hearts, when the Holy Spirit in our hearts speaks to us.

One day, when Jesus' disciples had watched Him pray, they said, "Lord, teach *us* how to pray." They knew that God is very great, and they did not know just how to pray to Him. Jesus told them to pray like this:

Our Father which art in heaven,
Hallowed be thy name.
Thy kingdom come.
Thy will be done in earth, as it is in heaven.
Give us this day our daily bread.
And forgive us our debts, as we forgive our
  debtors.
And lead us not into temptation, but deliver us
  from evil:
For thine is the kingdom, and the power, and
  the glory, for ever. Amen.

That is how we should pray—*first* praising God, *then* asking Him for the things we need, and then *praising* Him again.

SOMETHING TO TALK ABOUT:

Let's read the Lord's Prayer again, and talk about the things Jesus told us to pray for.

142

Shall we learn the first part of this prayer?

Our Father which art in heaven, Hallowed be thy name.

MATTHEW 6:9

SUGGESTED READING:
Philippians 4:6, 7

HYMN

Here are two verses we can pray while we sing them:

Blessed Father, great Creator,
Humbly at Thy feet we bend;
To Thy throne for all Thy favor
Youthful praises now we send.
Blessed Father, blessed Father,
To our youthful songs attend.

Blessed Spirit, great Consoler,
Make our hearts Thy dwelling place;
Teach us, guide us, sanctify us,
And console us all our days.
Blessed Spirit, blessed Spirit,
Ever cheer us with Thy grace.

PICARDY
(CH 20; HY 131; JS 7)

A PRAYER:

Dear Father in heaven, we praise You because You are so very great and wonderful. It makes us happy to tell You all about ourselves. Please give us what we need today, and take care of us in the night. We thank You for all the good things we have, and for the fun we have when we play. And we thank You for listening to us. Help us to listen to You, and to praise You. *Amen.*

Praying
in Jesus' Name

Do you know the story about Queen Esther?
Esther was a beautiful queen. And she was one of God's people, the Israelites. But the king, Ahasuerus, was not one of God's people.

One day, Ahasuerus' wicked servant, Haman, wanted to kill all God's people. He hated them. And the king told wicked Haman he could do *whatever* he wanted to. The king liked Haman.

Esther's uncle, Mordecai, heard what Haman was going to do. He and all God's people were very sad. But Queen Esther did not know about it.

When Esther heard that her uncle was very

sad, she sent a servant to ask him what was the matter. He told her what Haman was going to do. And he said to Esther, "You are a queen. *You must go to the king and ask him not to let Haman do this.*"

Mordecai thought maybe God had made Esther queen just so she could do this.

Esther was *afraid* to go to the king. She said to Mordecai, "The king does not want *anybody* to come unless he tells the person to come. If I go to him, I will surely die, unless he holds out his golden scepter to me."

But there was no other way to save God's people. So at last Esther did go to the king. Oh, she was so *afraid*. But when the king saw her, he was *pleased*. He smiled, and held out his golden scepter to her. He said, "What is it you want, Queen Esther?"

Then Esther asked the king to help her, and she saved her people.

If Esther was afraid to go to the king, who was only a *man*, *we* ought to be afraid to go the great King of kings, who is Lord God over *all* the earth and heaven. And we *are* afraid when we remember how great and holy God is, and how small and sinful *we* are.

But we do not *have* to be afraid—not if we go to Him the *right way*. God has *made* a way for us. His way is much more wonderful than the golden scepter that Ahasuerus held out to Queen Esther. We can go to God in *Jesus' Name*. Do you remember how Jesus once said to His disciples, "I am the way"? He is the *only* way to God. We can go to God only in His Name.

Besides that, Ahasuerus was a cruel and wicked king. God is kind and loving.

One day Jesus said to His disciples:

Whatsoever ye shall ask the Father in my name, he will give it you (John 16:23).

That is a wonderful promise.

What does it mean to pray to God in Jesus' Name? It means that we believe that Jesus died for us. It means that our sins are forgiven for Jesus' sake.

It means, too, that our hearts are filled with love for Him, and we will ask only the things that please Jesus.

When we pray to Him that way, the Father is *glad* to have us come to Him.

SOMETHING TO TALK ABOUT:

What is the only way for us to go to God?
What shall we ask for today?
How shall we use these things to praise Him?

SUGGESTED READING:

Philippians 2:9–11

HYMN

Here is a hymn about the Name of Jesus:

At the name of Jesus
Every knee shall bow,
Every tongue confess Him
King of glory now;
'Tis the Father's pleasure
We should call Him Lord,
Who from the beginning
Was the mighty Word.

KING'S WESTON
(HY 106, 141)

A PRAYER:

Great and holy God in heaven, we cannot come to Thee except in Jesus' Name. But oh, we are so glad that Jesus died for us! Now we know Thou wilt forgive our sins and hear our prayers. Help us to ask and to want only what will please Thee and our precious Lord Jesus. *Amen.*

144

Where
We Should Pray

Solomon was a very wise king. He was very rich, too. He built a beautiful Temple for God.

God called that Temple "the house of prayer."

When the beautiful Temple was finished, King Solomon called all the Israelites to come to Jerusalem.

What a happy day that was! People crowded the streets of Jerusalem. They all went up the hill to see the beautiful Temple. They brought sacrifices to burn on an altar as presents for God. They sang His praise. And they *prayed*.

The people all prayed together. King Solomon stood where all the people could see him. He lifted his hands to heaven. He said, "Lord God of Israel, there is not a God like Thee, in heaven above or on earth beneath." He *praised* God with *all* his heart.

Then the king knelt down before God. He led the people in prayer, and he prayed a *long* time. He had so much to say to God, and to ask of God! He asked God to bless His people, and to bless this beautiful *house of prayer*.

Today we do not have a temple. We have *churches*. Sometimes we call our *church* a "house of prayer." We know that God is there, and that He *hears* us when we pray to Him there.

But we can pray to Him in other places, too. We can pray when we are at home. We can pray in school. We can even pray while we are playing, or while we are walking down the street.

God is *everywhere*. No matter *where* we are, we can pray to Him.

Church is a special place of prayer, because in church God's people pray *together*. God likes to have His people come together to pray to Him.

Sometimes you pray with Mother and Daddy. A whole *family* can pray together. It is wonderful for a whole family to love God together, and pray to Him together!

But you can pray *alone*, too. *Wherever* you are, you can pray. God hears your prayer, no matter *where* you are. You will want to pray alone especially at night, kneeling by your bed, with only *God* seeing you. You remember how Jesus prayed at night, kneeling in the dark.

SOMETHING TO TALK ABOUT:

What did Solomon do when he finished building the Temple?

Why did he call all the people to come?

When do we pray together?

Where did you pray alone, today?

MEMORY VERSE

Paul wrote to his helper, Timothy:

I will therefore that men pray every where, lifting up holy hands.

I TIMOTHY 2:8

SUGGESTED READING:
I Kings 8:22–24, 26–28

HYMN:

> The same great God that hears my prayers
> Heard His, when Jesus knelt to pray;
> He is my Father, who will keep
> His child through every day.

CHILDHOOD
(CH 100)

A PRAYER:

Father, even though we are very small, You will hear our prayer—wherever we are. Help us to remember to call upon You every time we need something; and help us to praise You in prayer whenever we think how great You are. *Amen.*

How We Should Pray

Do you fold your hands and close your eyes when you pray?

That is a *good* way to pray. When we fold our hands, we keep them from doing what they should not do while we are talking with God.

When we close our eyes, we keep them from seeing what they should not look at while we pray. We fold our hands and close our eyes so that we will think *only* about God, and about what we are *saying* to Him.

But maybe sometimes we will want to pray *without* closing our eyes and folding our hands.

Nehemiah was one of God's people. He lived in faraway Persia. He was a servant of the king of Persia. He had to bring wine to the king.

One day a brother of Nehemiah came to visit him. Nehemiah asked him about God's people and God's city.

The brother said, "The people are very poor, and in trouble. The walls of Jerusalem are broken down. The gates are burned with fire."

Then Nehemiah was very sad.

When Nehemiah went to the king, to bring him his wine, the king said, "Why do you look so sad, Nehemiah? Is your *heart* sad?"

Nehemiah said, "I cannot help looking sad, O King. The city of my people is all broken down, and the gates are burned with fire."

The king said, "What would you like to do?"

Then Nehemiah prayed. *Right there*, while he stood before the king, he prayed to God. He could not kneel then, or fold his hands and close his eyes. He just *stood* there. He asked God to make the king kind and good.

And while he prayed, he said to the king, "If it please the King, I would like to go to my country. I would like to help my people build the city."

And the king *let* Nehemiah go. God *heard* Nehemiah's prayer. The king even sent soldiers to go with Nehemiah.

God made the king kind and good, in answer to the prayer that Nehemiah prayed while he talked to the king.

Nehemiah did not pray that prayer *aloud*. He prayed it *in his heart*. Only God could hear it. The king did not hear it at all.

We, too, can pray *in our hearts, without* folding our hands and closing our eyes. We can pray while we are playing. We can pray when something happens *all at once* to frighten us.

We ought to pray that way *very often*.

Sometimes we *kneel* when we pray. Sometimes we sit down. But we can even pray when we walk, and when we work. Much praying will make us *happy* Christians.

SOMETHING TO TALK ABOUT:

What does it mean to pray *in our hearts?*
Why should we sometimes kneel to pray?
How can prayer make us happy?

JESUS SAID:

Ask, and ye shall receive, that your joy may be full.

JOHN 16:24

SUGGESTED READING:

Psalm 95:1–6

HYMN:

Blest Spirit, one with God above,
Thou source of life and holy love,
Oh, cheer us with Thy sacred beams,
Refresh us with Thy plenteous streams.

O holy Father, holy Son,
And Holy Spirit, three in one,
Thy grace devoutly we implore,
Thy name be praised for evermore.

O HEILAND,
REISS DIE HIMMEL AUF
(HY 107)

A PRAYER:

Dear Jesus, we thank Thee for hearing *all* our prayers. No matter where we are, we can pray to Thee in our hearts. How wonderful and good Thou art! *Amen.*

What We May Ask For
in Prayer

There are so many things we like to have! May we ask God for *anything* we want?

Of course, God's children will never ask Him for *bad* things. We will never ask God for things we *know* are not good for us.

We may ask Him for anything we need, and for anything we like, if we think it is good for us.

The Bible tells a story about King Hezekiah, who lived long ago. King Hezekiah was a good man. He loved God, and tried to do His will.

One day a wicked king came to make war against Hezekiah. He had a very strong army. He said he would take *everything* that Hezekiah had. He wanted to take even God's city, Jerusalem, and say it was his.

Hezekiah trusted in God. But the wicked king sent a letter to Hezekiah. In the letter he said, "Don't trust your God. Your God cannot save you. My big army has made war with many other people. They prayed to *their* gods, but their gods could not save them. And *your* God cannot save *you*."

Hezekiah thought how big and strong the army of the wicked king was. He knew his army was not strong enough to fight the kings. So he went to the Temple to pray, to ask God to help him. He knelt down in the Temple, and he spread the letter open for God to read.

Hezekiah prayed, "Look, O Lord. See what the wicked king says about You. All that he says about other gods is true. They did not save their people. They *could* not, because they were *idol* gods. But You are the *living* God, the *only* God. Oh, help and save us!"

God was pleased with Hezekiah's prayer. He *did* save Hezekiah, and the city, and all His people. He sent an angel to frighten the wicked king and his army. That night all the soldiers ran away.

God wants *us* to tell Him *our* troubles. He wants *us* to ask Him for help. Remember, He is our *Father*. Your Daddy opens his arms when you run to him for help. Our Father in heaven opens *His* arms, too, when we go to Him in prayer.

He wants us to ask Him for anything we need, and even for the things we would like to have, when we do not really need them.

SOMETHING TO TALK ABOUT:
What have you asked of God today?
What has He given you?

THE BIBLE SAYS:
Pray one for another.

JAMES 5:16

What does that mean?

SUGGESTED READING:
II Kings 19:14–19

HERE IS A BEAUTIFUL HYMN:

> What a friend we have in Jesus,
> All our sins and griefs to bear!
> What a privilege to carry
> Everything to God in prayer!
> Oh, what peace we often forfeit,
> Oh, what needless pain we bear,
> All because we do not carry
> Everything to God in prayer!
>
> Are we weak and heavy laden,
> Cumbered with a load of care?
> Precious Saviour, still our refuge;
> Take it to the Lord in prayer.
> Do Thy friends despise, forsake Thee?
> Take it to the Lord in prayer;
> In His arms He'll take and shield Thee;
> Thou wilt find a solace there.
>
> CONVERSE
(JS 171)

PRAYER

(Shall we pray for ourselves, and for others too?)

Dear Father in heaven, we thank Thee for our Lord Jesus, our dearest Friend. We are glad that we can ask Thee for anything, and come to Thee with all our troubles in His name. Help us to pray only for good things—the things that can please Thee. *Amen*.

How God Answers Our Prayers

"Mother, may I have an apple?" Do you ever say that? Or, "Daddy, can we go for a ride?" We ask so *many* things of Mother and Daddy!

Do Mother and Daddy always let us *have* what we ask for? Oh, no! Sometimes they think it's better for us *not* to have what we ask for.

Sometimes they cannot *afford* it. Sometimes they *cannot* give it.

Neither does God always give us what we ask for.

God *can* give us what we ask for, but He does not always do that.

There are many reasons why God does not always give us what we like to have.

If we ask God for something when we have been *naughty*, and when our sin is not *forgiven*, then He does not hear our prayer. We must *first* ask Him to forgive our sins.

Sometimes we ask for things just for our own *fun*. God does not like *such* prayers either. Do you remember what He says about being selfish? If we think just about what *we like*, we are *selfish*. God does not want us to be selfish, and He does not hear selfish prayers.

Sometimes God does not give us what we ask for even though *we* think we need it very much. Paul, the great missionary, had a "thorn." It was not a *real* thorn. It was something that bothered Paul very much. Maybe it was pain in his eyes. We do not know. Paul asked God to take that "thorn" away. He prayed about it three times. Paul thought he could be a better missionary if God would take the "thorn" away and make him well.

But God did *not* take the "thorn" away. God said it was *better* for Paul to *keep* it! So God did not give even Paul what he asked for.

Paul was not unhappy about this. Paul knew it was *best*. Paul knew that God *always* does what is best for His children.

Daddy and Mother try to do what is best for us. Very often they do not give us what we ask for, because it would not be *good* for us. God knows, even *much better* than Daddy and Mother, what is good for us and what is not good for us. Even *Jesus* prayed, "Not *My* will but *Thine* be done."

God *always* hears us when we pray. But He does not always give what we ask for. Sometimes He says, "No; that is not good for you." Sometimes He says, "Wait. You cannot have it

yet." If it is good for us, He will give it. We must learn to *trust* God.

SOMETHING TO TALK ABOUT:
What did we ask of God today?
Did we ask something selfish?
Did we ask for forgiveness of our sins?
What does it mean, to trust God?

WE READ IN THE BIBLE:
My God shall supply all your need.
PHILIPPIANS 4:19

When we live close to God, He will give all that is good for us.

SUGGESTED READING:
Psalm 66:16–20

HERE IS A HYMN ABOUT GOD'S WAY:
What God ordains is always good.
He is my Friend and Father;
He suffers naught to do me harm,
Though many storms may gather.
Now I may know
Both joy and woe,
Some day I shall see clearly
That He hath loved me dearly.

What God ordains is always good.
This truth remains unshaken.
Though sorrow, need, or death be mine.
I shall not be forsaken.
I fear no harm,
For with His arm
He shall embrace and shield me;
So to my God I yield me.
WAS GOTT TUT
(HY 38; JS 140)

A PRAYER:
Dear God, You are very great. You can give us anything we ask. But we often ask for foolish things and things that would not be good for us. Help us to trust You. Give us what we need, and make us very thankful, for Jesus' sake. Help us to pray for others as well as for ourselves. *Amen.*

The Most Important Prayer

God wants us to ask Him for the things we need. We need food and clothes and a house to live in. These things are important. But there is something even more important—*much* more important.

One day Jesus climbed a green hill with His disciples. He sat down on the grass and called His disciples to come and sit close around Him. Birds were chirping and singing. Some were catching insects in the air; some were running on the ground, looking for worms and bugs. Little flowers lifted pretty faces in the green grass. It was a beautiful day to sit outdoors and listen to Jesus.

First Jesus told the disciples how blessed and wonderful it is to belong to God's Kingdom. "Blessed are the poor in spirit," He said, "for they shall inherit the earth." And "Blessed are the peacemakers." And "Blessed are the pure of heart."

Then He talked about how God's children must *live* for God, what they must be like, and what they must do.

Jesus said, "You must not worry about having enough to eat or enough clothes. Look at those little birds. Your Father in heaven feeds them, and you are worth much more than the birds. Surely He will feed *you*.

"And look at the flowers. See how pretty they are. Your Father in heaven gives them petals much prettier than any clothes the rich king Solomon ever had. Surely He will clothe *you*." He loves us, you know.

Then Jesus said, "You should not always be thinking about clothes and about money. Such things don't last. They wear out, or rust away, or are eaten by moths. People who do not know God are always thinking about those things. There is something much more important: *Seek ye first the Kingdom of God*."

When Jesus taught His disciples to pray He said they should ask: *"Thy Kingdom come"* (Matthew 6:10). Praying for God's Kingdom is more important than asking for our bread, or clothes, or anything else we need. Praying for God's Kingdom is the *most important* prayer of all. And Jesus said that if we put the Kingdom *first*, we will get everything else we need! That's His promise!

What do we ask for, when we put God's Kingdom first? We can ask God to make *us* bright little candles to shine for Him. We ask Him to bless the missionaries so that more and more people will come to love Jesus. We can pray for boys and girls who do not know Him, who do bad things. Can you think of other things to ask?

Let's never forget that most important prayer of all, "Thy Kingdom come."

SOMETHING TO TALK ABOUT:

Why is the Kingdom of God so important?

Who is our King when we belong to the Kingdom of God?

How can we show, in our play and in all we do, that God is our King?

SUGGESTED READING:

Matthew 6:25–33

HERE IS A HYMN TO SING:

"Seek ye first the kingdom, 'tis your
Father's will;"
So the voice of Jesus bids us follow still.
Saviour, we would hear Thee, follow, find,
and see;
And, in life's adventure, Thy disciples be.

As for hidden treasure, or for matchless
pearl,
When at last discovered, men will sell their
all;
So, when breaks the vision of that
kingdom fair,
Ours shall be its riches and its beauty rare.

KING'S WESTON
(HY 106, 141)

A PRAYER:

Our Father which art in heaven, Thy Kingdom come. Bless every minister and missionary
and teacher who tells the story of Jesus, and help
me to tell it too. For Jesus sake, *Amen*.

MEMORY VERSES OF PART TWELVE

Our Father which art in heaven, Hallowed be they name.
MATTHEW 6:9

Whatsoever ye shall ask the Father in my name, he will give it you.
JOHN 16:23

I will therefore that men pray every where, lifting up holy hands.
I TIMOTHY 2:8

Ask, and ye shall receive, that your joy may be full.
JOHN 16:24

Pray for one another.
JAMES 5:16

My God shall supply all your need.
PHILIPPIANS 4:19

Thy Kingdom come.
MATTHEW 6:10

152

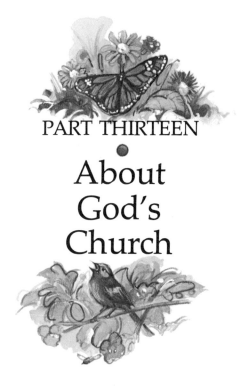

PART THIRTEEN

•

About
God's
Church

Why We Go
to Church

Do you remember how long God worked to make heaven and earth and everything we see around us? Yes, He worked *six* days. He made the trees and all other kinds of plants, the birds and other animals, and last of all, man. He made everything in six days.

Then came the seventh day. All God's work was finished. And on the seventh day God *rested*. He rested, and He *enjoyed* looking at all the things He had made.

Do you remember the lesson about the creation of man? How God made man in His own image? Man was made to be *like* God. And so God wants *man* to have a day of rest, just as *God* had a day of rest. And that day of rest is man's day to *enjoy* all that God does for him.

God called this day of rest the Sabbath day. And that day is so important that He gave a commandment about it in His law. The commandment says: *Remember the sabbath day, to keep it holy. Six days shalt thou labour and do all thy work; But the seventh day is the sabbath of the Lord thy God.*

This day of rest is good for us. God was not tired after making heaven and earth and everything else, but *we* get tired when we work hard. If we did not have a day of rest, we would get *very* tired. God knew we would need a day of

rest. He was good to us when He told us to rest one day in seven.

But our Sabbath is much more than just a day of rest. It is a day of *joy*. It is a day to think about God, and to be happy with all that He has given us and all that He has done for us. It can be a wonderfully happy day of *praise* to God.

Our Sabbath means even more than *that*. God tells us that on our Sabbath day we should remember a *promise* He made. God has promised to give us another Sabbath, an even *better* Sabbath. It is a Sabbath that shall *never* end. That wonderful Sabbath will come at the end of time, when God takes us all to be in glory with Him. Then *all* our hard work will be done. And then we shall enjoy God *forever*. That wonderful Sabbath will be in heaven.

Sunday is our Sabbath now, our day of rest. We call it the *Lord's* day, because the Lord Jesus did especially wonderful things for us on that day. It was on Sunday morning that Jesus arose from the grave. It was on a Sunday morning that He sent the Holy Spirit down to live in the hearts of His people. And so we go to church on Sunday, to praise God, to worship Him, and to listen to His Word. It is a day of happiness.

God's people of long ago sometimes forgot to keep the Sabbath day holy; they forgot to make

154

it God's day. They just had a good time on that day. They made it a day for their *own* joy. They did not have joy in the *Lord*. Isaiah, the great prophet, told them they should honor the *Lord* on His day.

SOMETHING TO TALK ABOUT:
Why do we call Sunday the Lord's day?
How can we be happy in the Lord on that day?
What does our Sabbath tell us about a coming Sabbath?

MEMORY VERSE
This is what Isaiah said about the Sabbath day:

Then shalt thou delight thyself in the Lord.
ISAIAH 58:14

SUGGESTED READING:
Matthew 28:1–8

We should not do what God's people of long ago did. We want to remember to make the Sabbath day a day of joy in the Lord. It is *His* day.

HERE IS A HYMN ABOUT THE SABBATH:

This is the day the Lord hath made;
He calls the hours His own.
Let Heaven rejoice, let earth be glad,
And praise surround the throne.

Hosanna in the highest strains
The Church on earth can raise;
The highest Heavens, in which He reigns,
Shall give Him nobler praise.

GRÄFENBURG
(CH 42)

A PRAYER:

We thank Thee, Father in heaven, for our day of rest. And O Lord Jesus, help us to make Thy day a very special day of joy and praise. When we remember all that Thou hast done for us, and when we think of the wonderful Sabbath that is coming, we thank Thee with all our hearts. *Amen*.

How We Worship God in Church

On Sunday you wear your very best clothes. You are as clean as can be. You look very neat and nice. And then you go to church.

Why do you wear your very best clothes on Sunday? Why do you wash yourself so clean and nice? And why do you go to church?

You can worship God at *home*. You can be *happy* in the Lord at home, on the Lord's day.

But we go to church to worship God *there*. God has told us that He is *pleased* when we come together in His house to worship Him. And he has promised to be *there* with us. Of course we wear our *best* clothes when we go to meet Him there. The Bible tells us that in the *eternal* Sabbath, when we shall worship God in glory *forever*, we shall wear *white* robes, pure and beautiful, to show that all our sins are washed away.

How do we worship God in church? We worship Him first by being quiet. We *want* to be quiet, so that we can *think* about Him and all His wonderful works, especially His work of *salvation*. And we worship God by singing praises to Him. And we worship Him in *prayer*. We pray silently, in our hearts, each one alone. And we pray *together*, when the minister talks to God.

We worship God with our *gifts*, too. God will use our money. He uses it to help other people. He uses it to send missionaries to tell the story of Jesus to people who do not yet know Him. We are *glad* to give our gifts to Him, because we *love* Him.

And we worship God by *listening* to what He says to us. *He* speaks to us when the minister reads the Bible, and when he explains the Bible. The minister tells us about God and His wonderful Kingdom of Heaven. He tells us how God wants us to trust and obey Him. If we listen to God's Word, and take it into our hearts, God is *pleased*, and He will bless us.

When we have really worshipped God, we go home *happy*.

When Jesus was a boy, He went to the Temple one day. He loved the Temple, because it was His Father's house. In the Temple Jesus found some men who loved to talk about God. Jesus listened. He wanted to hear them talk about His heavenly Father, because He loved His Father so much. Jesus listened, and sometimes He asked questions. And He forgot to go home! After a while His father and His mother came to get Him. They were surprised to find Him talking with these great men!

We should want to learn all about God. He is so wonderful!

When we go to church, we should listen carefully. We should sing and pray. We should think about Jesus and His great love for us.

SOMETHING TO TALK ABOUT:
How do we worship God in church?
What does God do for us there?
What can we do to please God?

MEMORY VERSE
There is one very *special* reason for going to church. *Jesus* is there. He once said:

Where two or three are gathered together in my name, there am I in the midst of them.

MATTHEW 18:20

SUGGESTED READING:
Psalm 122

Dear Lord, here in Thy house of prayer
We come to worship Thee;
Help us to feel that Thou art near
Our little words of love to hear,
As we sing joyfully.

LOBT GOTT IHR CHRISTEN
(CH 43; JS 24)

When we dress in our very best on Sunday, Father, let it be to honor Thee. And when we are in church, help us listen to Thy Word carefully. Help us to sing and pray from hearts that love Thee. Then we will honor Thee, and please Thee, and be happy in Thee. *Amen.*

Baptism

Just before He went up to heaven, Jesus told His disciples to go and tell *everybody* about Him. He also said that they should *baptize* all who would believe on Him.

There are three special things that the minister of a church must do. He must *preach* God's Word, telling people about Jesus. He must *baptize*. And he must also serve the *Lord's Supper*.

All three help us to learn more about God, and to grow more and more like Jesus. That is what every Christian must do!

Baptism helps us because it is a *sign*. It shows us that Jesus cleans our hearts.

We use water to wash our faces and our hands. We bathe our bodies in water. We need water to make ourselves clean.

We need the blood of Jesus to make our *hearts* clean. We need the blood of Jesus that He gave when He died on the cross.

When the minister baptizes someone in water, that is a *sign* to *show* us that Jesus washes our hearts. Baptism says: Just as *water* makes your body clean, so Jesus' *blood* will make your heart clean if you believe on Him.

And baptism is a sign that God makes us *new creatures*. The Bible says that when we are baptized we are *buried* with Jesus, and we *rise* with Him to a *new* life. You remember the story— how Jesus died, and was buried, and then *arose* from the grave with a wonderful new body. When we believe in Jesus, the Holy Spirit makes *us* new; He gives us new hearts that love God and want to do His will. And someday, when Jesus comes back, we shall have new *bodies*, too—heavenly bodies, to live forever with God.

God *promised* that. And baptism helps us see that God's promise is *sure* and *true*.

Do you remember the story of Philip and the man who rode in a chariot? As soon as the man believed in Jesus, he *wanted* to be baptized. And then he went on his way happy, because he was *sure* that he belonged to Jesus.

There is a story in the Bible about a man who was baptized in the middle of the night. The jailor at Philippi was a cruel man. One day officers brought Paul and Silas to him. They told him to keep them locked up tight. So he put Paul and Silas in the *worst* part of the jail. But that night he was frightened by a terrible earthquake. *Then* he asked Paul what he had to do to be saved. Paul said, "Believe on the Lord Jesus Christ." And the jailor *did* believe! He was sorry for his sin. And he received a new heart. Then Paul baptized him and all his family, in the middle of the night.

Baptism reminds us of God's great love. God the Father promises to make us His children and forgive us our sins. God the Son gave His blood to wash away our sins. God the Holy Spirit lives in our hearts to make us pure and holy. All three Persons work together to make us ready for heaven. That is why the minister says, "I baptize you in the Name of the Father, and of the Son, and of the Holy Ghost."

SOMETHING TO TALK ABOUT:
What does the minister do when he baptizes someone?

What does he say?
What does the baptism mean?

JESUS SAID:
Baptizing them in the name of the Father, and of the Son, and of the Holy Ghost.

MATTHEW 28:19

SUGGESTED READING:
Acts 16:28–34

HYMN:
Baptized into Thy name most holy,
O Father, Son, and Holy Ghost,
I claim a place, though weak and lowly,
Among Thy seed, Thy chosen host.
Let naught within me, naught I own,
Serve any will but Thine alone.

O DASS ICH TAUSEND
(JS 98)

A PRAYER:
Lord Jesus, if You do not wash away my sin, I can never go to heaven to be with You. We thank You for telling Your disciples to baptize. We thank You for the sign that helps us believe that we can be washed clean even though we are very sinful. *Amen.*

The Lord's Supper

Baptism helps us believe that our sins are washed away and that we really belong to Jesus. And if we really belong to Him, we may have *supper* with Him. We may sit at the *Lord's* table.

All of God's people, all over the world, eat the Lord's Supper. Jesus *told* us to do that.

Just before He died, Jesus and His disciples had supper together. While they were sitting around the table, Jesus took bread and broke it. He gave each of His disciples a piece.

Jesus said, "Take it, and eat it. This is *my body*, which is given for you."

The disciples all ate the bread. But they did not understand what Jesus meant.

After that, Jesus took the cup of wine. He blessed it. Then He said, "This is my blood, which is shed for many. All of you must drink of it." And each of the disciples drank a little.

The very next day, Jesus died on the cross. In the Lord's Supper He had *shown* His disciples that He was giving His body and His blood for His people. He gave His body and His blood on the cross.

When Jesus arose from the grave, the disciples *understood* about the bread and the wine. Then they knew that Jesus had died for them.

Today God's people eat the bread and drink the wine to *remember* that Jesus died for them. The bread and wine help us understand and help us believe that Jesus *really* gave His body and His blood for us when He died on the cross. It is a sign. Just as we take bread and wine to feed our bodies, so we take Jesus into our hearts to give us eternal life.

When children grow up and give their hearts to Jesus, and love Him, *they* may eat the Lord's Supper, too. That will be a sign for them that they too, belong to Jesus, and that He died for them.

The Lord's Supper is a sign for others, too. It tells others what we believe. When God's people eat the bread and drink the wine at the Lord's Supper table, they are showing others that they believe Jesus died for them. And they are showing others that they *belong* to Jesus.

When you really try, with all your heart, to live for Jesus, people can see that you belong to Him. And when you are old enough to go to the Lord's Supper, you, too, will show others that you belong to Him and that He died for you.

SOMETHING TO TALK ABOUT:

What do we remember at the Lord's Supper?

Why did Jesus give us this sign of the Lord's Supper?

When may boys and girls eat of the Lord's Supper?

MEMORY VERSE

The Church calls us to the Lord's Supper because Jesus said:

This do in remembrance of me.

LUKE 22:19

SUGGESTED READING:
I Corinthians 11:23–26.

HYMN

When God's people eat of the Lord's Supper, they think about Jesus. Here is a hymn they sometimes think about and sing:

O dearest Lord, Thy sacred head
With thorns was pierced for me;
Oh, pour Thy blessing on my head
That I may think on Thee.

O dearest Lord, Thy sacred hands
With nails were pierced for me;
Oh, shed Thy blessing on my hands
That they may work for Thee.

ALBANO
(CH 118)
or DETROIT (KENTUCKY HARMONY)

A PRAYER:

Jesus, we thank Thee for the Lord's Supper, because it tells us of Thy great love. It should make us happy deep down in our hearts. We praise Thee, and sing glory to Thy Name because of Thy great love. *Amen*.

Bringing Others to Church

Do you remember what Jesus said just before He went to heaven? He told His disciples to go and tell *all* the world about Him.

If *we* are happy in Jesus, we want others to be happy in Him, too. If we are happy worshiping God in His house, we will want others to come *with* us to worship Him.

Andrew and John were Jesus' first disciples. They followed Him one day when He walked near the river. When Jesus saw them, He invited them to come to where He lived. That day He talked with them about the kingdom of heaven.

How Andrew and John listened! They had never heard such wonderful news. They had never listened to such a wonderful man!

When it was time for Andrew and John to go home, Andrew hurried to find his brother Simon.

"Simon!" he said, "we have found the Christ!"

The Christ? Simon could hardly believe that Andrew had found the *Christ*. The people of Israel had been waiting and waiting, for many *long years*, for Christ to come. Now, all of a sudden, Andrew said, "We have *found* Him!"

When Simon could not believe it, Andrew said, "Come with me. I will bring you to Him!"

Simon went along with Andrew, and *he* heard Jesus talk about God and His Kingdom. And then he, too, believed that Jesus was the Christ.

Simon was *glad* that Andrew had told him about Jesus and taken him to Jesus. Both Andrew and Simon, and John too, became disciples of Jesus.

If *we* know Jesus, and love Him, we want *others* to know Him, too. God has made us happy by showing His great love to us. And we want to make *others* happy in Jesus. He is the greatest man that ever lived!

Besides that, everybody *ought* to love Jesus. Everybody ought to love and worship God, and obey Him. We were made for Him, to please Him. People who do not love Jesus are not pleasing God. We want them to come to church to learn all about God, and how they ought to live for God.

SOMETHING TO TALK ABOUT:

Why did Andrew bring Simon to Jesus?

How can boys and girls bring others to Jesus?

THE BIBLE SAYS:

Every tongue should confess that Jesus Christ is Lord, to the glory of God the Father.

PHILIPPIANS 2:11

When we bring others to church, we will ask the Holy Spirit to work in their hearts, so that they will believe.

SUGGESTED READING:
John 1:44–51

HERE IS A HYMN ABOUT BRINGING PEOPLE TO JESUS:

From utmost east to utmost west,
Where'er man's foot hath trod,
By the mouth of many messengers
Goes forth the voice of God;
Give ear to me, ye continents,
Ye isles, give ear to me,
That the earth may be filled with the glory
   of God
As the waters cover the sea.

PURPOSE
(HY 151)

161

A Prayer:

Father in heaven, all people ought to love and serve Thee. Thou art great and holy. Thou hast made us for Thyself. But so many, many people do not know Thee! Bless the missionaries who go out to tell about Thee. And show us how *we* can bring people to Thee, so that they may learn to know and love Thee, too, for Jesus' sake. *Amen.*

MEMORY VERSES OF PART THIRTEEN

Then shalt thou delight thyself in the Lord.
ISAIAH 58:14

Where two or three are gathered together in my name, there am I in the midst of them.
MATTHEW 18:20

Baptizing them in the name of the Father, and of the Son, and of the Holy Ghost.
MATTHEW 28:19

This do in remembrance of me.
LUKE 22:19

Every tongue should confess that Jesus Christ is Lord, to the glory of God the Father.
PHILIPPIANS 2:11

PART ONE
•
Looking
For
God

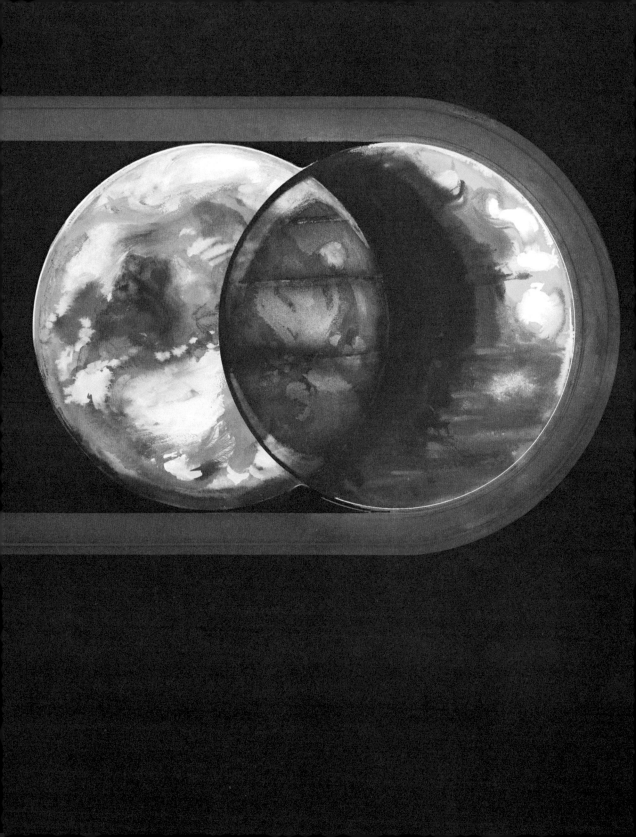

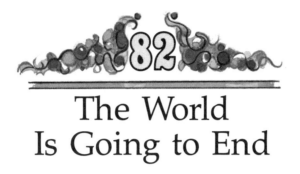

The World
Is Going to End

Do you remember that everything had a *beginning*? The very first words of the Bible tell us: *In the beginning God created the heaven and the earth*.

Heaven and earth will have an *ending*, too. God has told us so in the Bible.

One day Jesus' disciples were looking at the beautiful Temple in Jerusalem. They said to Jesus, "Come and see how very beautiful the Temple is."

The Temple was made of big white stones, and trimmed with shining gold. There were big pillars and high towers. There were wide porches, with benches where people could sit. Oh, it was all so beautiful! The disciples *loved* the Temple.

Jesus went with them to look around. But He was sad.

Jesus said, "Do you see all these things? Listen, I will tell you something. All this is going to be broken down. Not *one* stone will be left on top of another."

That made the disciples sad. They did not like to think that someday the beautiful Temple would be broken down. They thought that if the Temple was broken down, surely that would be the end of the world.

But the Temple *was* broken down, not many years after Jesus went to heaven, by the army of a cruel king.

The Bible tells us that another day is coming when the world will come to an end. All that we see around us will pass away. It will be burned with fire.

We feel sad when we think of this. And we feel *afraid*. It will be a terrible day.

The Bible calls that day, when the world will come to an end, *the great and terrible day of the Lord*. On that day the Lord Jesus will send fire from heaven, to destroy all that is sinful. The fire will burn up the earth. All the wickedness of Satan and of sinful people will be burned, too. And Jesus will be Lord over all.

On that day *everybody* will know that God is much greater than Satan. Everybody will see Jesus and His angels. And they will fall down before Jesus. Then they will know that He *really is* Lord of lords and King of kings.

All the *wicked* will be afraid. They will cry out. It will be a *terrible* day for them—a day of punishment for their sin.

But God's *children* need not be afraid at all! They will *not* be punished for their sins. And God will save them from the fire. He *never* lets anything harm His dear children.

And He will make a *new* heaven and a *new*

earth for His children, where they will live to serve Him forever.

SOMETHING TO TALK ABOUT:

Why will God destroy the earth with fire?
Why is this day called the great day of the Lord?
Why need God's children not be afraid?

MEMORY VERSE

This is what the Bible says about the end of the world:

The earth also and the works that are therein shall be burned up.

II PETER 3:10

SUGGESTED READING:
II Peter 3:10–13

HYMN

Even though the world will end one day, this hymn reminds us that Jesus will protect us:

The Lord's my shepherd, I'll not want,
He makes me down to lie
In pastures green, He leadeth me
The quiet waters by.
He leadeth me, he leadeth me,
    the quiet waters by.

Yea, though I pass through shadowed vale,
Yet will I fear no ill;
For Thou art with me and Thy rod
And staff me comfort still.
Thy rod and staff me comfort still,
    me comfort still.

Goodness and mercy all my days
Will surely follow me;
And in my Father's heart alway
My dwelling place shall be,
And in my heart forevermore
    Thy dwelling place shall be.

BROTHER JAMES' AIR

A PRAYER:

Father, we are afraid when we think of the terrible fire that will burn up the earth. But we know the fire will burn up only evil. We need not be afraid. Help us to trust Thee. And on that great day we shall see Thy greatness and Thy wonderful glory. And we will praise Thee more than ever before. *Amen.*

Jesus Is Coming Back

Do you remember how Jesus went to heaven? He was up on a mountain with His disciples. He held out His hands to bless them. And then He went up—up—up.

The disciples wondered. What was He going to *do*? They saw Him go higher and higher. Then a cloud came. The cloud *hid* Jesus, so that they could not see Him any more.

The disciples kept looking up. They thought maybe they would see Him once more. If only the cloud would go away!

And then, all at once, two other persons were there standing by the disciples. These men wore shining white clothes. They were *angels*.

The angels said to the disciples, "Why do you keep looking up: Jesus is going to come *back* again, *just* the way He went up. He will come back on a cloud."

Then the disciples were glad.

But they did not stay on the mountain to *wait* for Jesus to come back. Oh, no! They remembered what Jesus had told them. There was work to do for Him. They had to tell the story of Jesus to other people.

Many, many years have gone by since Jesus went to heaven. And He has *not* come back yet.

But He *said* He would come back. And the *angels* said He would come back. Jesus always keeps His promises, you know. He *will* come.

When will He come?

Before He went away, Jesus told His disciples that the *whole* world must hear the gospel story. He said He would not come back until *all* nations know about Him. And He told *us* to go out and tell the nations, all people *everywhere*, about Him.

We have *work* to do while we wait for Jesus to come back. It is the most important work in all the world. We must tell the story of Jesus and His love. We must tell sinners to go to Jesus and be made clean. We must be missionaries. And we must *send* missionaries.

When all our work is done, Jesus will come again. He will come to take all His dear children home, to the Father. Then God's *whole* family will be together in heaven. How wonderful that will be!

When we think of this, we can hardly wait. We pray, "Lord Jesus, come quickly!" We get ready to meet Him. And we work to gather in His children from every land.

When we think how wonderful it will be in heaven, we do not care so much for the things on this earth. We think most of what we can do for Jesus, and how we can get ready for His coming.

SOMETHING TO TALK ABOUT:

What shall we do while we wait for Jesus to come?

What kind of work can we do for Him?

THE BIBLE SAYS:

For we are labourers together with God.

I CORINTHIANS 3:9

SUGGESTED READING:

Revelation 1:4–7

In these verses John tells us how he saw Jesus in heaven, ruling over the earth.

HYMN:

Lo! He comes with clouds descending,
Once for favored sinners slain;
Thousand, thousand saints attending
Swell the triumph of His train:
Alleluia! Alleluia!
Christ the Lord returns to reign.

Yea, amen! Let all adore Thee,
High on Thine eternal throne;
Saviour, take the pow'r and glory;
Claim the Kingdom for Thine own.
Oh, come quickly! Oh, come quickly!
Alleluia! Come, Lord, come!

PICARDY
(CH 20; HY 131; JS 7)

PRAYER

(Shall we read the second verse of the hymn, and make it our prayer?)

167

What Will Happen When Jesus Comes?

One day Jesus told a story about a farmer who sowed good seed in his field. When the farmer had finished his work, and was gone away, an enemy came. The enemy sowed *weed* seeds.

After a while the good seed began to grow. But the *weed* seeds grew, too.

The farmer's men went out to look at the field. They saw the weeds among the good

plants. They hurried to tell the farmer. They asked him, "Didn't you sow good seed?"

"Yes, I did sow good seed," the farmer said. "An *enemy* came and sowed the weed seeds."

Then the men wanted to pull the weeds out. But the farmer said, "No; just let them grow together. If you pull up the weeds, you might pull up the good plants, too. When *harvest* time comes, we will pull out the weeds, and we will burn them. And then I will gather the good wheat into my barns."

Jesus' disciples asked Him the meaning of that story. They knew it was a *parable*—an earthly story with a heavenly meaning.

Jesus said, "The field is the world. The *good* seeds are the children of God. The *weeds* are the children of Satan. Satan is the enemy who sowed them. They grow *together* now. God's children and Satan's children live side by side."

The harvest is the end of the world, and the reapers are the angels. The Son of man shall send forth His angels. They shall be like the reapers who gathered all the weeds, to burn them. But the children of the Kingdom He will take *home*, to be with the Father.

When Jesus comes, the people who *would* not love Him and obey Him will be very, very sorry. God will send them into outer darkness, where Satan will be. There they will be *very unhappy* forever. That is sad.

But God will take His people to heaven. The Lord Jesus will come *suddenly*, on the clouds, and all His holy angels will be with Him. There will be a great shout, and a *trumpet* will blow. And *all* the people on earth will see Jesus.

Even the *dead*, in the cemeteries and everywhere, will waken. They will come out of their graves. They will *live* again, and they will see Jesus.

Then those who did *not* love Him will be afraid. They will try to hide. But those who *did* love Him, and who *do* love Him, will be very, very happy. And He will take them up, to meet Him in the clouds. From wherever you are, at home or at school or at play, He will take you up suddenly if you belong to Him. Those who came out of their graves, if they loved Him, will go up with Him, too. They will have *new* bodies. All God's children will have new bodies—wonderful *spiritual* bodies that are fit for heaven.

What a wonderful day that will be! No wonder we look and pray for that day to come soon!

SOMETHING TO TALK ABOUT:
Which two kinds of people are on earth now?
What will Jesus do with them when He comes?
Will you be afraid when He comes?

THE BIBLE SAYS:
The Lord himself shall descend from heaven with a shout.

I THESSALONIANS 4:16

SUGGESTED READING:
I Thessalonians 4:16,17

HYMN:
Brothers, this Lord Jesus
Shall return again,
With His Father's glory
With His angel train:
For all wreaths of empire
Meet upon His brow,
And our hearts confess Him
King of glory now.

KING'S WESTON
(HY 106, 141)

A PRAYER:
Lord Jesus, what a wonderful day that will be, when we see Thee come on the clouds, and when we go to meet Thee! O Father, help us every day to get ready for that great day. *Amen.*

If I Should Die

Jesus is coming back, and it will be wonderful to meet Him in the clouds. But maybe we will not *live* till the day He comes. Maybe you will have to *die* before He comes. Maybe *I* will have to die. Old people die. Sometimes boys and girls die.

Peter and James and John, and the great missionary Paul, they all looked for Jesus to come back. They prayed that He would come while they were living. They thought maybe *they* would be on earth to hear the shout and see Him come. But they *died*.

169

God thought it was best that way.

And maybe He will think it best for *us* to die. But that does not really matter at all. Our bodies will have to be buried, in a grave in the cemetery. But our *souls* will go to heaven! Your body is only a house—the house your soul or spirit lives in. Your soul, your spirit, the *real* you, will go right to heaven if you are one of God's children. And when Jesus comes again He will raise your body out of the grave and make it a *new* house, a new *body*.

Thousands of God's children have died. Their souls are in heaven now, with Jesus. They are happy there. And they are waiting for that won-derful day of the Lord, when Jesus will give them new *bodies*.

When Paul, the missionary, was an *old* man, he was put in prison for preaching about Jesus. But even in prison he did all he could to tell the wonderful story of salvation. And he wrote let-ters to the churches, reminding the people to be true to Jesus and love Him.

One day Paul wrote a letter to his friend Tim-othy. He told Timothy that his work was almost done. He said he knew God would soon come to take him home to heaven. And he said he was *eager* to go. Paul *wanted* to die.

Do you know why?

This is what he wrote in a letter to one of the churches:

Having a desire to depart, and to be with Christ; which is far better (Philippians 1:23).

Oh, yes we may be happy down here on earth. God has given us so much to make us happy—so many good things! But to go to heaven and be with Jesus will be far better, *much* better!

So we need not be afraid to die. If we are God's children, we will go to heaven and see our dear Saviour. What a happy day that will be!

SOMETHING TO TALK ABOUT:
Why should we not be afraid to die?
In what ways will our bodies be changed? When will that happen?

THE BIBLE SAYS:
We shall all be changed.

I CORINTHIANS 15:51

A HYMN TO SING:
For all the saints
    who from their labors rest,

Who Thee by faith
    before the world confessed,
Thy name, O Jesus, be forever blest.
Alleluia! Alleluia!

Thou wast their Rock, their Fortress,
    and their Might;
Thou, Lord, their Captain
    in the well-fought fight;
Thou, in the darkness drear,
    their one true Light.
Alleluia! Alleluia!

But lo, there breaks
    a yet more glorious day;
The saints triumphant rise in bright array;
The King of Glory passes on His way.
Alleluia! Alleluia!

SINE NOMINE
(JS 82)

A PRAYER:
O Lord Jesus, how we ought to love Thee! Make us obedient and loving children. Then we will not be afraid to die. Then we will be happy to go to heaven and see Thee, dear Jesus, and be with Thee forever. *Amen.*

Praise to God Forever

Do you remember *why* God made the heavens and the earth? Yes, He made them for *His* glory. He made *everything* for His own praise and His own pleasure—the stars in the sky, the birds that sing, the flowers—everything should praise Him. All *people*, too. *Everybody* should praise Him, because He is the great and holy God, the God who *made* all things, who *cares* for all things, and who *loves* us.

Everything *did* praise Him in the beginning

before sin came to spoil His wonderful creation.

And some day everything will praise Him *again*!

The Bible tells us that wonderful things are going to happen, and after that, *everything* will praise and honor God again.

When John, one of Jesus' disciples, was an old man, he was put on a lonely island. Wicked men made him live there so that he could not go around telling people about Jesus.

One day, when John was there alone, something *wonderful* happened. *Jesus* came to him. John *saw* Jesus—a shining and glorified Jesus, the way He is now in heaven. It was a *vision* that John saw. It was like a dream.

John fell right down on his face when he saw Jesus in all His glory. But Jesus put a hand on John and said, "Do not be afraid. I am He that lives and was dead. And I am alive forevermore."

Then Jesus showed John things that are going to happen. John wrote everything in a book. We can read all about John's vision in the last book of the Bible, the book called Revelation.

Some of the things John saw were *dreadful*. Sin and Satan and all the wicked people and the people who do not love and serve God were punished. But Jesus showed John that after all these dreadful things have happened there will be *glorious* things. And at last heaven and earth will be *full* of God's glory!

John saw a *new* heaven and a *new* earth. And he saw a beautiful city coming down from heaven—a new Jerusalem.

Then John heard a voice that said, "See, God is coming to live with His people! He shall wipe away all tears. There will never be any more sorrow, or sickness, or pain, or death!"

John tells us that he saw the new Jerusalem, bright and shining with God's glory, and with beautiful sparkling jewels. And it did not need sunshine or moonlight, because God and Jesus are the light of the city. And there will be no night at all. There will be only light and joy and happiness, and praise to God forever.

When John saw all this he prayed, "Come, Lord Jesus!" He could hardly wait for the wonderful things really to happen.

And when *we* think of all the wonderful happiness that is coming, and how we shall share in God's glory, we too pray, "Come, Lord Jesus!"

SOMETHING TO TALK ABOUT:
When will God come to live with us?
How will everything praise God?

JESUS SAID TO JOHN:
Behold, I come quickly.

REVELATION 22:12

SUGGESTED READING:
Revelation 21:1–7

A HYMN TO SING:
Through north and south and east and
    west,
May God's immortal name be blest:
Alleluia, Alleluia!
Till ev'rywhere beneath the sun
His kingdom comes, His will is done.
Alleluia!

Praise God from whom all blessings flow;
Praise Him all creatures here below;
Alleluia, Alleluia!
Praise Him above, ye heav'nly host:
Praise Father, Son, and Holy Ghost;
Alleluia!

LASST UNS ERFREUEN
(CH 6; HY 7; JS 83)

A PRAYER:

O God, how great Thou art! How we ought to praise Thee! Oh, make us truly Thy children, to praise Thee forever, and to share in Thy glory, when there is no more sin and everything praises Thee, on the new earth and in the new heaven, for Jesus' sake. *Amen*.

MEMORY VERSES OF PART FOURTEEN

The earth and the works that are therein shall be burned up.
II PETER 3:10

For we are labourers together with God.
I CORINTHIANS 3:9

The Lord himself shall descend from heaven with a shout.
I THESSALONIANS 4:16

We shall all be changed.
I CORINTHIANS 15:51

Behold, I come quickly.
REVELATION 22:12